THE
DIGITAL
DISTRIBUTOR

ISBN (paperback) 979-8-849-61244-7.

First Edition 2022.

Edited by Vincent Czyz.

Published by
Modern Distribution Management, a publication of Gale Media, Inc.
6309 Monarch Park Place, 201
Niwot, CO 80503

About
Modern Distribution Management

Modern Distribution Management (MDM), a Gale Media Company, is a market research and media company that provides business intelligence resources to executives in wholesale distribution.

Since 1967, MDM has been the industry's most trusted, reliable and definitive media resource for distribution management best practices through its market research, analytics, publishing and conferences.

By delivering credible and unbiased news and business intelligence, Modern Distribution Management is the leading provider of guidance on how distribution executives can innovate, gain a competitive edge and build thriving businesses.

Visit us at www.mdm.com.

THE DIGITAL DISTRIBUTOR™

Six Steps to Accelerate Sales

Susan Merlo

Endorsements

"As a distributor we are struggling with the developing of an introduction or invitation to see customers face-to-face. This book provides insight and an easy-to-understand pathway for us to transition quickly into a more digital interface/marketing connection with our customers. I can see how these digital tools will lead us to introductions and invites for face-to-face meetings at the right point in the sales process. Great timing Susan!"

Jim S. Banovich
CEO, Marsh Electronics

"Susan Merlo has created an essential read for marketing (and sales) leaders throughout distribution. Throughout the book Susan shares the latest in B2B marketing and supports it all with case studies from distribution companies; and unlike most others, she prescribes the very next step you must take to market in a post pandemic world (with downloadable worksheets!) One other thought, for those who "get it" but struggle helping others see the reality of marketing in the digital age, buy this book for every leader in your company and lead a discussion on its topics. You'll move the needle!"

Dirk Beveridge
Founder, UnleashWD

"What I like most about this book are the carefully laid out step-by-step guidelines for developing an online marketing and sales plan. Using digital technology to strengthen existing customer relationships and to find new customers is rapidly evolving. Distributors who have yet to embrace digital technology will find this book actionable and easy to digest. This is a DIY approach that includes all the collateral material, downloadable from the publisher's website, required to facilitate an in-house project. The processes described in this book are thought provoking and will challenge you to rethink how to find and keep good customers. The sales and marketing strategies that helped get your company to where it is today will likely need to change with the times. Leveraging the approach outlined in this book will surely help your company continue its successful journey."

Ken Brown
Managing Partner, Evergreen Consulting

"A kind of technological revolution is afoot within distribution. The COVID-19 pandemic has served as a catalyst for rapid technological growth, pushing the world further into the digital sphere than ever before. Truly, "distribution is on the cusp of metamorphosis" - and accelerate it will!

Change is more top of mind than ever. Customers demand, among other things, robust options to interact with their suppliers and robust order fulfillment practices. This change will ultimately influence your company's future.

Wholesale distributors still mired in the "conventional wisdom" are challenged with how marketing and sales will need to interact to compete online and what ownership/senior management should possess in the way of new expectations for the future.

So, along comes Susan Merlo and her new book! Susan has surely laid out a clear and detailed roadmap to change. She's identified the core elements that will best position distributors for change, and she's provided workbook exercises and very digestible instruction.

It's a major step up from other books I've recently read on this topic. Highly recommended!"

Howard W. Coleman
Principal, MCA Associates

"The pandemic changed your customers. We must accept that.

- They shop differently.
- They buy differently.
- They think differently.

Are you ready to run your business to meet those changes?

Whether you are aligning your sales and marketing teams, learning more about your buyer personas, or re-examining your marketing automation projects, the time is now to take a new approach to learning more about your current customers and engaging new ones.

Susan Merlo's new book sharpens all of those rough edges, cleans up any past misconceptions, and allows you to hit a reset button when it comes to not just talking to your customers, but communicating with them so you can receive the feedback you need to grow today and throughout this decade.

There is always some fear when it comes to making large scale changes, especially when it comes to sales and marketing. But Susan's book will ease those fears when you realize the buy-in from everyone in your organization is simple and easy to understand, thanks to the workbook format this book provides.

Someone told me a few years ago that he wasn't sure he wanted to be the first one to make major changes, but he definitely didn't want to be the last. You don't want to wait to solidify your sales and marketing strategies. This book will provide a step-by-step path into the future, and it will make sure you don't finish last."

Scott Costa
Publisher, tED Magazine

"Susan provides indispensable insights and executable actions for immediately growing sales and delighting customers, and at the same time, building a foundation for B2B innovations and the future of distribution.

This book is a must read for every distributor leader and rising star!"

Mark Dancer
Author, Mark Dancer on Innovating B2B
CEO, Network for Business Innovation

"The pandemic has forced a sense of urgency to leverage digital capabilities to grow your business. The age of acceleration is upon us! Susan presents a robust roadmap for distributors to compete online effectively. As a distributor, if you are unsure where to begin, Susan's framework is a compelling starting point. A must-read book that is packed with several tools to get you started immediately. If you are a distributor that has kickstarted your digital transformation, the checklists in the book will help you reach your goals faster. Susan has done all the hard work for you. It's time for us to get moving."

Pradip Krishnadevarajan
Co-Founder, ActVantage and NAW Author

"Susan has written her second book addressing how to start a sales transformation process. I recently forwarded a prepublication draft of the book to a client CEO. He read it over the weekend and put an immediate halt to his team's purchase of a new CRM package. It was the right thing to do. His team felt the pressure to start their own sales transformation but didn't know what they didn't know. This book prevented them from making a large mistake.

This book does not cover the already well-traveled ground about why change is necessary. We are all deluged with the 'change now or die' message in social media and trade publications every day. More importantly, this is a book of six steps that examines how *to start and how the pieces fit together. It provides very tangible and specific examples of what the new normal will look like for an industrial distributor."*

Mike Marks
Managing Partner, Indian River Consulting

"Susan's new book is a how-to roadmap for creating an effective, New Normal, digital-marketing capability. Most distributors are good at putting customers into standard channel segments. But Susan's distributor case studies illustrate how to further refine segments into actionable personas that will make marketing collateral and decisions more effective.

For the CEOs and owners of small firms, this will be an eye-opening education and will give you the insight into who you must hire and what they must do. Mid-to-larger distributors with marketing staff should use Susan's book to audit, upgrade, update and transform existing capabilities. Read and discuss the steps to uncover historic frustrations and exciting new possibilities."

D. Bruce Merrifield, Jr.
President, Merrifield Consulting

"We all have our 'secret sauce' of how we help customers, and this playbook gives you simple, step-by-step instructions on what we all need to be doing so that we as distributors can communicate our value to more people. Susan's book accomplishes what many

distributors have wrestled with for years, specifically: How do we let more people know about all the amazing things our teams do for our customers?

Follow Susan's compass, and you will find your distribution company surrounded with more customers for whom you are a better fit to help solve their problems."

Brian R. Peters
President, Peters Supply, Inc.

"*Susan Merlo's* The Digital Distributor: Six Steps to Accelerate Sales *is an excellent roadmap for distributors to follow as they look to accelerate their digital transformation. I have personally worked with Susan for the last two years while launching our digital marketing initiatives at Building Products Inc. She is a wealth of knowledge, and distribution leaders would be wise to follow her six steps as they look to innovate their sales and marketing strategies for the future.*"

Kyle Schull
President, Building Products Inc.

"*After reading the book, distributors and wholesalers should be able to implement some of the digestible instructions Susan included in this book. I couldn't put it down. It saves so much time with its roadmap approach.*"

Nelson Valderrama
CEO, Intuilize

"Over the last 20 years, I have led digital transformation for some of the largest distributors in the US, and I can tell you firsthand how much a resource like The Digital Distributor *is needed. Many distributors' marketing organizations are still focused on event planning, branch promotions and very basic email and web marketing.*

In order to compete and win, you have to leverage the massive amounts of data that distributors have access to and turn that into targeting strategies to engage and retain customers. This book provides the blueprint to leverage best-in-class digital marketing practices that can transform a distributor."

Keith Williams
Founder & CEO, Factrees

Dedication

This book is dedicated to my cherished friend and sometimes mentor, Steve Epner, whose guidance helped tremendously in getting this party started.

In case you're wondering whatever happened to the book, Steve, here it is. More bagels coming soon!

And a special thank you to Mike Marks and Tom Gale for recognizing this book as the missing link for distributors facing a digital sales transformation journey; and to Mike Kunkle for confirming the importance of these six steps in the first few chapters of his outstanding book on sales enablement. It's great to know that I'm not crazy.

Contents

Foreword

The leaders of industrial distributors today recognize that the industry is in the middle of massive changes. Customers are changing how they source, there are now four generations in the workplace, manufacturers are going direct (disintermediation), disruptors from outside the industry are seeking growth in this market, and digital is everywhere. According to Forrester Research we lost almost 25% of the 4.2 million B2B sales reps in the US between 2015 and 2020, replaced by inside sales and digital. If that wasn't enough, throw in a pandemic.

Susan has written her second book addressing how to start a sales transformation process. I recently forwarded a prepublication draft of the book to a client CEO. He read it over the weekend and put an immediate halt to his team's purchase of a new CRM package. It was the right thing to do. His team felt the pressure to start their own sales transformation but didn't know what they didn't know. This book prevented them from making a large mistake.

This book does not cover the already well-traveled ground about why change is necessary. We are all deluged with the 'change now or die' message in social media and trade publications every day. More importantly, this is a book of six steps that examines how to start and how the pieces fit together. It provides very tangible and specific examples of what the new normal will look like for an industrial distributor. You will understand what this is all about when you see the examples; it isn't that tricky when you scape out all the intergalactic BS.

We have a well-established practice within Indian River in digital sales transformation and work with many of the industry's leading distributors. We provide Susan's book to those distributors that are just starting on their journey to provide them a framework of what they are required to design and build BEFORE they acquire a CRM package or make any other investment. It is not about selling stuff on the web.

As this massive change is happening very quickly in the industry there are few real experts. If you have responsibility to make this transition in your own firm, it is important that you become one of these experts.

This book provides the reader with a solid beginning and a foundation to begin the journey. For most, the journey takes longer than a full year, even moving with speed.

In the beginning it is overwhelming to most, so it is unbelievably valuable to know how to start. The transition is hard enough without having to back up and start over.

Enjoy the ride.

Mike Marks, Founding Partner
Indian River Consulting Group

Preface

We are now well into the 21st century, and it's clear that
innovation and digital technology are critical to the success of
almost any company—perhaps *every* company. Ignoring this aspect
of business means risking that your competitors who invest in the
latest technological advances to connect and stay connected to their
customers will one day gain an insurmountable advantage. Moreover,
the world is facing extraordinary challenges, and both time and
resources are in short supply.

A significant amount of B2B product selection and purchasing
has moved to the internet, and so your marketing collateral plays a
much larger role in capturing, directing, and keeping your prospects'
attention. In fact, it's often your marketing collateral that moves new
customers closer to a purchase, educating a buyer before passing
him to sales for closing. Taking that into account, now more than
ever it's time for you to focus on your company's digital sales and
marketing strategies and ensure your strategies are positioning you
to succeed in this space.

In 2012 and throughout the five years following, the NAED (National Association of Electrical Distributors) published a series of 18 Executive Guides written to support leaders in distribution companies who want to strategically plan, execute, and then manage their company's online presence. Even if you are not an electrical distributor, you can still benefit from these guides since their advice would be helpful to *all* distributors. If you haven't done so already, I highly recommend you look at these NAED publications.

One of the guidebooks describes how roles in the IT and marketing departments are changing in the distribution industry. It also talks about how mobile technology, social media, and e-commerce will be changing the way distributors communicate, interact, and conduct business. It emphasizes that the demand for real-time information is mushrooming since people do their research and make their purchasing decisions online and no longer wait for a knock on the door from a salesperson.

Despite the guidance put forth by the NAED and other resources like it, many distributors have been holding off on employing any digital sales and marketing strategies and tactics. This is understandable. After all, the distribution industry continued to do well conducting their sales via good old-fashioned face-to-face interactions.

But then things changed. Our country found itself in the midst of a pandemic with no end in sight. No doubt, you and your employees were affected both personally and professionally. And it is very likely that your ability to rely on traditional methods to communicate with your customers, find new customers, and build or strengthen important customer relationships was hit hard. A new normal quickly emerged in the distribution industry.

This new normal has accelerated your customers' acceptance and future likelihood of doing more buying activities digitally. New thinking and new processes will be necessary to strengthen your presence in the marketplace and remain competitive and able to stay in touch with your customers.

By the way, your customers *do* want you to stay in touch. The difference is, they'd like you to communicate with them on *their* terms.

This book will show you what *their* terms are, and it will help bridge the gap from old sales practices to new by walking you through exercises, examples, and strategies. You will learn from stories of how other distributors have handled their digital sales and marketing challenges. You will also be able to pick out what you think will work for your company and use the forms and exercises throughout the book to make it easier for your team to adapt and adopt new ways.

Do your best to be patient; the changes you put in place are necessary, and they will require an investment of time and resources. And there's no need to panic—better to take your time and do it right the first time than have to do it over.

Introduction

Someone once said the only person who likes change is a wet baby. Well distributors, it's time to get wet!

This book was written to prepare you for a much-needed sales transformation—more specifically, to prepare you for the digital sales and marketing strategies you must undertake, which has been necessitated by the changes that have taken place—and will continue to take place—in the industry.

I've been consulting with distributors, sharing the information contained in this book for years; and yet, throughout those years, many have chosen to skip several of these steps. The truth is, before now, it didn't matter because, as I said earlier, distributors did incredibly well at face-to-face sales. Digital sales and marketing was a nice-to-have, not a must-have.

Today, that's no longer the case. The six steps in this book are one hundred percent necessary if you are going to succeed at building a strong, sustainable online presence. I cannot stress this enough. If you've already begun putting your digital sales and marketing strategies together, please page through the table of contents to ensure you didn't miss any of the steps included. If you're not sure about which steps to act on first, call me, and we'll figure it out together.

The steps you are going to walk through will keep your sales efforts nimble and innovative. These same steps will ensure prospects and customers find your website, find the products and solutions you offer, and learn about the value you provide. These steps will ensure website visitors keep coming back. And, if you have invested in eCommerce, you will see an increase in your return on that investment.

You'll find your company better equipped to take advantage of new technologies, especially those relevant to digital sales and marketing strategies, once you have completed the exercises I'm sharing here. We'll go through each of the steps necessary to create a strong, stable, and lasting online presence.

Completing the activities laid out for you will require time and resources, but the tasks will not be overwhelming. You will be given all the tools and guidance necessary to keep moving forward. For each activity you will be provided with supporting downloadable worksheets and checklists. These supplemental materials will help break down each exercise into bite-sized, digestible chunks that will build upon each other.

Why It's Necessary to Prepare for a Sales Transformation

There's a high level of product research and purchasing taking place online today. Your digital sales and marketing collateral will be playing a vital role in attracting and driving customers through your sales funnel. Completing the adventure you're about to embark on will ensure your buyer's journey is positive, targeted, frictionless, and successful. With the industry's shift toward digital, embarking on this adventure is more important than ever.

I cannot emphasize enough that, because digital sales and marketing strategies are so easily available to all, *now really is the time to move forward* and start reaping the benefits and leapfrogging your competition.

You won't see changes overnight, but you will feel change coming almost immediately, and you will better understand the importance and long-term benefits of each step you are guided through. You will also feel much better prepared for *anything* the future of digital sales and marketing holds for the industry.

Since COVID hit, we've still not seen any indication that sales practices will go back to what they were. It's quite the contrary, in fact. And at the very least, digital sales and marketing strategies will remain one of the most efficient ways to becoming more competitive.

The six steps this book will take you through will form a foundation for all your company's digital sales and marketing efforts going forward. Consider the contents of this book your 'roadmap to success' as you successfully move through all six steps in the prescribed order.

The six objectives or milestones we will hit together are:

- The alignment of the efforts and goals of your sales and marketing teams (including incorporating them into a unified vision of the company and its sales mission)
- The clear and unequivocal understanding of who your customer segments are and what each segment's goals and challenges include
- Sales and marketing messaging that clearly communicates the value your company offers to each customer segment

- The ability to deliver your messaging to each customer segment; in other words, getting the right message to the right customers at the right time in the right format

- A system that drives, captures, and nurtures your leads, measures a lead's value, and knows when to pass each lead to sales for closing

- An ability to develop a fuller, more accurate picture of your digital efforts' effectiveness and ensure you're generating maximum value without spending additional marketing dollars

Who This Book is For

This book is written for distribution company executives and sales and marketing leaders *to prepare your company* to succeed online. It cannot be stressed enough that all six steps are necessary if your company is going to be equipped to take advantage of new technologies, especially those relevant to digital sales and marketing strategies.

As you move forward, you'll find that your sales and marketing teams will come away with a better understanding of what each should be doing in conjunction with the other to build a stronger digital presence together. The teams will learn, step-by-step, how to lay the groundwork for future success.

When all six objectives mentioned above are in place, rest assured your business will gain new customers and you'll increase customer retention and wallet-share. Your efforts will attract more eyes to your website and produce better-qualified leads for your salespeople. Not only will the actions I'm recommending drive up sales, but they are well within any organization's ability to implement.

Take your time as you move forward. Each lesson builds upon the next, and the knowledge you pick up in each chapter will be applied in more than one exercise.

Make good use of the Supplemental Worksheets, Checklists, and Agendas available for each exercise. Most of the documents are interactive, and each will guide you smoothly and quickly through the exercises in this book. Once completed, the worksheets will serve as re-usable tools that your sales and marketing teams can refer to for many years to come.

Visit MDM.com/TDDBook to download
the Worksheets, Checklists, Agendas, Guidebooks, etc.
referred to in this book.

CHAPTER 1

Aligning Your Sales and Marketing Teams

"A Fortune 250 B2B company spent a quarter of a million dollars trying to solve the wrong problem. A new product line had failed, and the company believed the problem was either poor product delivery times or lack of effort by the sales force. After throwing millions at both problems, they finally realized what the real issue was: misaligned goals between marketing and sales."[1]

Historically, in most distribution companies the marketing team has been tasked with creating materials that compel buyers to learn more about the services and products the company offers, with the sales team focused on face-to-face sales.

In fact, the distribution industry has been so successful with this model that it's enjoyed the luxury of being one of the *last* industries

---

1   Reprinted by permission of *Harvard Business Review*. From "When Sales and Marketing Aren't Aligned, Both Suffer" by Ritz, Wendy, Steward, Michelle D., Morgan, Felicia N., and Hair, Jr., Joseph F. June 2018. Copyright ©2018 by Harvard Business Publishing; all rights reserved.

to welcome digital strategies into their sales processes. While other industries have been forced to rely heavily on providing online content to help guide a purchase, distributors are just now beginning to move in that direction because today, the sales function in distribution is in trouble.

Buyers are hard to reach. Your salespeople can no longer call on new businesses like they used to. And even for verticals where in-person visits are encouraged, salespeople are often spread too thin. Your customers are not as dependent on your salespeople as they used to be.

Marketing materials that called for buyers to "get in touch with us for more information" are not as effective because buyers, it seems, would rather not "get in touch." Instead, buyers want real-time information with the click of a button, and they know that if they look hard enough, they will find what they want on the internet without having to call you.

To stay competitive and in touch with their audiences, many distributors are learning how to move as much of the sales process online as possible (note, this is not about eCommerce). Because your first line of communication starts with your marketing collateral, your ability to successfully remain top of mind in your industry requires a strong alignment of your sales and marketing teams.

Aligning the goals and vision of the sales and marketing teams presents a challenge or two, however. Traditionally, the marketing team has had long-range vision, while the sales team is more concerned with the short-term and has a greater sense of urgency. Sales and marketing teams throughout history, in every industry, have often been at odds because of these two teams having different goals. Nevertheless, alignment is attainable. And, with the two teams working together toward the same goals, your business will be much more competitive online.

This chapter will share the actual steps and strategies you can take to achieve alignment. It's a process that will span the entirety of this book, and by the end of the process, the two teams will be working well together, with each having a clear understanding of your company's sales goals and their respective responsibilities.

The 24-Hour Salesperson

Since our initial COVID-19 scare, most companies should have, by now, settled into new routines and habits. For the most part, it is likely your salespeople and most of your customers have found comfortable ways to keep in touch to some degree.

But consider when your customers look for products and solutions on the internet between meetings with their sales rep. A customer may pick up the phone and call you, but it's unlikely he'll call if he doesn't know your company offers what he is looking for, or if he feels he can find the information himself on the web. So, because of the average buyer's propensity to search on his own, you run the risk of customers discovering more comprehensive or helpful collateral from a competitor who offers the same or similar products and solutions as you do.

Take a look at the following situation.

Over the course of several years, a building-products distributor on the West Coast had a very profitable relationship with both Lowes and Home Depot to purchase the distributor's composite decking materials and some roofing materials as well. The big-box stores' orders and fulfillment cycles were basically on autopilot.

One day, the distributor's CEO, in reviewing his P&L, realized that, while sales of the roofing materials were increasing, composite decking sales to both stores were declining precipitously. Given that these were two of his most significant accounts, he decided to take matters into his own hands, starting with a call to the buyer at Lowes.

The buyer told the CEO that they, too, enjoyed their relationship with the distributor. "But," he said, "my hands are tied." He explained that he's been ordering composite decking for about four months now from a competitor, and his bosses were delighted with this new supplier. When asked why, the buyer explained to the CEO that his company's decking often arrived with chips and scratches, causing the product to either sit on the shelves for a long time or be returned mid-job. As a result, replacement decking was always on backorder, and contractors began shopping elsewhere. The big-box store eventually felt it best to go with a supplier who offered more reliable packaging capabilities.

"But we just spent five months building a new packing and staging area in our warehouse," the CEO explained. "We invested a fortune in new shrink wrapping and strapping machines to alleviate this very problem. Didn't you know?"

The buyer did not know. He'd told the distributor's sales rep about the problems months earlier, but that sales rep had moved on to a different company and never relayed the information.

After the call, the CEO called the other big-box store and informed their buyer about their investment in the new packaging systems. It was news to him as well. Luckily, the store was happy to give them another chance.

The CEO's next call was to his VP of Sales and Marketing, ordering him to have the marketing department print up literature about their new packaging systems and get it out to the salespeople.

"We did that months ago," said the VP, "but people just don't read that stuff." The CEO conceded the point. They agreed that creating more flyers and brochures, even blurbs on their website, would still be necessary, but they would have to find other, more effective ways to get the word out.

In the scenario above, the distributor sustained unnecessary losses because the sharing of important information to their best customers was left to chance. The company had a few paragraphs devoted to their new packaging capabilities buried on the Services page of their website, so it was much less conspicuous than it could have been.

And while the marketing team did a fine job creating a flyer about the new packaging systems, they weren't aware of the scratched decking problem their customers were experiencing. Had they known more about the situation, they could have created some digital marketing content that called attention to how their systems were solving this problem. Doing so would make information about the new packaging systems immediately discoverable wherever and whenever someone searched for a solution to the types of problems that stem from damaged shipments. The situation in which a distributor's own customers are unaware of the true value the distributor offers is relatively common.

Your marketing team knows that if your customers are looking for the solutions that your company provides, they must craft messaging that resonates with your customers, and promote the messaging so that your customers see it both on your website and in other places as well. Doing so ensures that your customers will know to look to you for their solutions versus gravitating towards a competitor's site.

Unfortunately, though, usually marketing teams in distribution are not as familiar with what customers are looking for or why. As a result, the services and solutions distributors provide often go unrecognized.

To remedy this, I've found that your messaging has a higher chance of reaching your target market when there is constructive dialogue taking place between the sales and marketing teams. Your marketing team's ability to create messaging that resonates with your existing customers will depend upon their having a better understanding of your customers and what your customers' goals, struggles, and needs may be. In other words, if gaining a more significant share of customer spending is something you'd like to see in *your* distribution company, aligning your sales and marketing team is imperative.

The same situation holds true for your prospects (the customers you haven't landed yet). As hard as it is for your salespeople to connect with existing customers, it's even more challenging to uncover new prospects. Since many buyers are working from home rather than in their offices, they are turning to the internet to get their problems solved and their educational needs met. The information your company publishes online, therefore, should be readily discoverable and worded so it resonates with prospects who are looking for answers. In doing so, the content you publish can be very effective in guiding prospects closer to a sale.

Aligning your sales and marketing teams is in the best interest of your organization. Eventually, if all goes well, you will be able to eliminate the gap between the information you *should* promote online and what you are actually promoting.

Having the sales and marketing team working closely together could be quite a big adjustment for everyone involved, and the alignment of the two teams can be tricky. Later in this chapter we'll go through the actual steps and strategies to take to align the two teams. By the end of the exercises laid out for you, the two teams will be working well together, sales will increase, and everyone will be much happier.

Laser-Targeting Your Ideal Customers

Your salespeople's time is more precious than ever right now, and it stands to reason that their time is best spent focused on the most lucrative prospects. When your marketing pieces are targeted directly at your ideal customers, your messaging will be more effective in attracting the right customers *and* deflecting the wrong (low-margin, less-profitable) customers. Marketing that deflects non-ideal customers can directly benefit your sales team because it will keep their focus on the more profitable customers. Here's an example of how that's done:

A gym-equipment distributor has, among others in its customer base, three distinct audiences for which they'd like to review their sales and marketing practices. The three segments they're looking at are:

- *Gym owners*
- *Institutions (i.e., corporations, hotels, large residential developers, and the like)*
- *Homeowners or one-off purchasers of equipment*

On the distributor's home page is a toll-free phone number inviting customers to call to speak to a salesperson. And because the distributor sells to all three segments mentioned above (among other audiences), there are pictures related to all their segments on their home page. In other words, the distributor's marketing is targeting all of its audiences equally.

As with most companies, this distributor generates greater profits on its higher-volume sales. So, of the segments mentioned above, the distributor of course wants its salespeople to focus on gym owners and institutions. But the marketing team must continue to attract the third as well.

Unfortunately, because the distributor is marketing the same way to all three segments, incoming calls from website visitors could just as easily lead to a low-volume, low-profit sale as a high-volume, high-profit sale. This is a problem because responding to the low-volume, low-profit calls is a poor use of the sales reps' time.

Could the marketing team have taken specific steps to ensure that only the first two audiences call the telephone number while still marketing effectively to the homeowners without having them call the sales team? Yes, they certainly could have.

The example presented above depicts a "let's promote this product to anyone who would buy it" approach, which is an ineffective strategy for a company that wants their salespeople to spend the bulk of their time on high-volume sales. If the marketing team had known that the sales team would prefer not to speak to homeowners, the marketing collateral could have easily directed high-volume purchasers to the telephone number while directing low-volume customers, (i.e., the homeowners), to a contact page or a B2C-style order form.

Imagine the positive impact you can enjoy when your marketing team understands how best to support the sales function, and your sales team has more input into the content and the leads generated on your website!

The example also illustrates why it's extremely important to focus your marketing message on your *customers* rather than on the products your company sells to them. It's to your advantage when your messaging is about who your customers are, what they want or need right now (vis-à-vis a problem or pain point or goal), and how your services, solutions, or products will help them solve their problem, resolve their pain point, or meet their goal.

In other words, when your messaging is framed around your customer and what they're struggling with or working toward, you will not only relate to them more intimately, but you will also have better control over the path you would like them to take through your sales funnels toward a purchase.

Your sales team devotes their time to selling products to people who want and need them. Their experience, combined with their relationships with your customers, gives them insight into the customers' needs. The better the customer relationship, the more tuned in the salesperson becomes.

But in most distribution companies, marketing teams aren't privy to the knowledge your salespeople develop from interacting with your customers, so the marketing team will not be as tuned in to the customers as the sales team is. It's not surprising then, that the marketing team almost always will create collateral that revolves around products (vs. the customers' needs), focusing on the features of the products and presenting one universal marketing message across the board no matter the audience.

When your sales and marketing teams are aligned, the collateral produced by your marketing team will connect your customers to solutions the way your salespeople ordinarily would. As an added benefit, your *customers* will be much more aligned with your messaging because they will recognize that it speaks directly to them. Targeted messaging helps express to your audience that your business understands their needs. Your customers will also see a sales process that is clear and aligned with everything they read in your messaging. While that sounds like a given, it's not always the case. Sometimes we see information on a website or in a brochure that a salesperson isn't aware of. We also see instances when a salesperson refers to a promotion for which he or she cannot find any supporting information on their website or from the marketing team.

Identifying and Eliminating Barriers

There's no doubt that barriers will arise and must be tackled as you work through aligning your marketing and sales teams. Overcoming these barriers is vital if you would like to advance your sales and marketing efforts, so let's talk about some of the most commonly encountered issues that can arise.

Sales and marketing teams traditionally strive for different results at different speeds, and that can be something of a barrier. We've all seen situations in which a sales department has a product or special line to promote and requests that marketing produce some collateral right away, but the production of the collateral takes longer than anticipated, resulting in a missed opportunity for the sales team. When this happens repeatedly, a wedge begins to form between the two teams. If the wedge becomes too large, the business may reach a point where sales does their job, and marketing does theirs, each at their own pace, in their own silos, and separate from the other.

A CRM system is often involved in the sales and marketing teams' alignment because a CRM is the perfect place to house information about customers and prospects that both teams will need if they are to do their jobs effectively. This could present another barrier since some salespeople cringe at the thought of a marketing person accessing their leads while other salespeople may prefer not to use a CRM at all. Salespeople may be fearful of losing their leads; they may prefer using their own system to keep notes and records; they may be hesitant to try new technology; they may even be afraid of becoming obsolete and losing their jobs. While their concerns are understandable, these concerns can constitute a barrier to both alignment and the prospect of new business for you that must be worked through.

Another barrier you may encounter is that aligning the sales and marketing teams can result in more work for the marketing team. There may be additional pressures placed on the marketing team as their work becomes more critical to the sales process. And while marketing team members will learn to think more analytically, they may have more accountability and responsibilities than before, which could present some unwanted pressure. There will also likely be a higher demand placed on their time. Lastly, if the marketing team is not tech savvy, it could take a while to get them up to speed with new and necessary technology. The burden doesn't have to fall entirely on the marketing team's shoulders, however. Some distributors will tap on the inside sales team or a sales assistant to handle the analytics or the tech and to help support the overall process.

How about your company? Are you prepared to overcome the barriers that may arise? To help you prepare, we've created the *Barrier Elimination Worksheet*, which will take you through a brainstorming exercise to help you identify and troubleshoot any barriers to your teams' successful alignment that may crop up. As each barrier is identified, you will be better prepared with a plan to address it.

Aligning the two teams will be a significant change for both groups, which may even result in a certain amount of disruption within the entire organization. Any barrier to change, however, will be worth overcoming if in the end it brings you positive results, especially now that you have an idea of what to expect and how to handle each situation.

Be sure to keep your *Barrier Elimination Worksheet* handy. New barriers will identify themselves as you move through the exercises that follow. This worksheet will help you anticipate any difficulties and figure out in advance how best to handle them.

Who Does What, and Why?

When you think about the responsibilities between marketing and sales, it seems fairly straightforward. Marketing ignites interest, while the sales team is responsible for getting people to make a purchase. Traditionally the responsibilities of the two teams have been broken down as follows:[2]

But this scenario is quickly changing. Because so much of B2B shopping and purchasing has moved to the internet, your marketing collateral plays a much larger role in capturing, keeping, and directing your prospects' attention. Your digital collateral will be

---

2   Reprinted by permission of *Harvard Business Review*. From "Ending the War Between Sales and Marketing" by Kotler, Philip, Rackham, Neil, and Krishnaswamy, Suj. July-August 2006. Copyright ©2006 by Harvard Business Publishing; all rights reserved.

what moves new customers closer to their first purchase and existing customers to make additional purchases.

The following chart depicts a more authentic lifecycle of a long-term loyal customer. Notice how much interaction customers have with digital sales and marketing collateral before, during, and after the sales process. Every item mentioned below plays a role in moving someone closer to their next purchase.

Digital Marketing Throughout the Sales Cycle

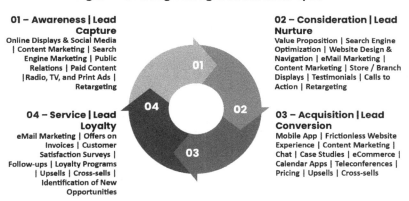

01 – Awareness | Lead Capture
Online Displays & Social Media | Content Marketing | Search Engine Marketing | Public Relations | Paid Content | Radio, TV, and Print Ads | Retargeting

02 – Consideration | Lead Nurture
Value Proposition | Search Engine Optimization | Website Design & Navigation | eMail Marketing | Content Marketing | Store / Branch Displays | Testimonials | Calls to Action | Retargeting

04 – Service | Lead Loyalty
eMail Marketing | Offers on Invoices | Customer Satisfaction Surveys | Follow-ups | Loyalty Programs | Upsells | Cross-sells | Identification of New Opportunities

03 – Acquisition | Lead Conversion
Mobile App | Frictionless Website Experience | Content Marketing | Chat | Case Studies | eCommerce | Calendar Apps | Teleconferences | Pricing | Upsells | Cross-sells

To clarify, the sales cycle, also known as the buyer's journey, is filled with touchpoints between your organization and your buyers. Most of these touchpoints result from material turned out by your *marketing* team, however. In other words, your marketing collateral either already plays or eventually will play a vital role throughout the entire cycle.

As you read through the items in the chart above, think about the prospects in your pipeline right now. When making buying decisions, an individual will often conduct as much research as possible. Their interaction with most of your digital collateral will be self-directed. Buyers will move through the various touchpoints at whatever speed and in whatever order is most comfortable for them.

Because a buyer's journey is no longer linear, you must include steps in your online sales funnels that ensure buyers do not stall or fall out of a funnel. Remember that buyers will often wait to get close to a final decision before picking up the phone to call a salesperson. For this reason, *a lot of buyer influence resides in the hands of your marketing collateral, so it makes sense for the sales team to get more involved in its creation.*

By producing collateral that deliberately moves your buyers closer to a sale, and by using tracking software and/or a CRM that keeps tabs on where each buyer is in the sales cycle, you will have a greater ability to capture and hold the attention of your buyers and guide each closer to a purchase. We'll discuss this in greater depth in Chapters Three, Four, and Five.

Your marketing team will not be able to produce effective digital collateral on their own. Marketing will need input from sales about each of your audience segments to design collateral that will move prospects from each segment closer to a purchase. Along those same lines, your salespeople will benefit from the information supplied by your marketing team about your prospects' movements and behaviors on your website. The sales team can keep tabs on which collateral is attracting which prospects and customers. They should also pay attention to information such as which customers and prospects clicked on which links, be it your product pages or a page devoted to your services and solutions. Having this knowledge will help prepare your sales team for their next interaction with the customer or prospect.

Both teams should know which prospects are taking action or moving more quickly through your sales funnels. And, both teams should also know which digital sales and marketing tactics are working, which are not, and why so that your sales funnels can be repeatedly refined. If your marketing collateral isn't generating enough new opportunities, or if the sales team isn't converting enough prospects into sales, it's important to see where the problems lie. Aligning the two teams and having them work together will be helpful in resolving any issues that are uncovered in the buyer's journey.

A lack of alignment between the two teams may result in finger-pointing when such problems arise. It may also result in substantial amounts of money being left on the table again and again.

Focusing on the Customer Experience

In 2019 I had a meeting request from a woman whose title was Director of CX. She was from a software company that had built a new ERP system, and she wanted advice on how to market to the distribution industry. Although at the time I had no idea what CX was, I took the meeting. After a few minutes of conversation, it finally dawned on me that CX was the cool new acronym for *customer experience*, and she was responsible for overseeing the company's customer experience. Moral of the story? Customer experience (CX) is important enough, in and of itself, to get its own slightly mysterious and somewhat cool acronym. And today we see it more and more.

Seriously though, the rising number of CX professionals we are seeing suggests that companies are spending money specifically to create an optimal experience for their customers. Part of *your* customers' experience is affected by what takes place during their buyer's journey. If the customer experience throughout your sales cycle is less than stellar, or if a customer's interactions with your sales and marketing materials fall flat, it's possible the sale will be lost. The same will hold true for customer interactions that take place in other areas of your organization as well.

For example, look at your website. Are visitors' anticipated questions readily answered? Is the information you provide engaging enough that your visitors will return at some point to learn more? Are customers locating helpful solutions to their problems in your content? If your company has an eCommerce site, are products easy to find? How about the checkout process? Is it easy to navigate? These are all issues you will learn to address and resolve as you move through this book.

Let's Get Started!

Distribution can take cues from other industries, many of which have taken significant strides toward integrating their sales and marketing departments. Some of the changes I've seen include marketing teams taking on new and more important roles and responsibilities. I've also seen inside sales teams contributing more to the collateral-planning processes.

Aligning your sales and marketing teams should kick off with a clear directive from your C-Suite. It's important to make sure that both teams understand the journey they are about to embark on is not about poor performance; rather, they're embarking on a journey that will *generate more sales*. Partnering the two teams can be a bit of a shock to both as well as to your company's culture; so, members of both teams, and perhaps other employees as well, are likely to be uncomfortable at first. Therefore, the full support of upper management is imperative to keep things moving in a positive light. You'll find that as the project progresses, the lanes of responsibility may seem to overlap, so having a solid set of deliverables, shared goals, and KPIs for all involved, including upper management, will help keep everyone on track.

Weekly or bi-weekly meetings with *pre-planned agendas* are advisable. It's best to be consistent with these meetings since maintaining momentum will go a long way toward bringing the project to fruition. If you miss a week here or there, the program may lose traction and eventually fall by the wayside.

If your marketing and sales teams are large enough, you might consider identifying just a few of your key players from each team to participate in the alignment. The participants will get more familiar with each other and eventually operate as one cohesive team as they move through the exercises together. And the more you can expose the teams to each other's workdays, the better. Sales will better understand marketing's points of view, and marketing will better understand where the sales team is coming from.

Neither team really knows what the other is dealing with or what the other team requires to get its job done. Their having this knowledge will become invaluable, both to the individuals on the two teams and to the rest of your organization.

From the outset, a useful goal to have in joining the teams together is to make sure both groups feel they are part of the same team.

The quote below from Jill Rowley, a fellow marketing expert, sums it up nicely:

> *"The new reality is that marketing needs to know more about sales, sales needs to know more about marketing, and we all need to know more about our customers."*

Ensure communications among the members of your newly formed team stay upbeat and as stress free as possible. Let everyone know that the alignment of the two teams will be better for the whole organization. Prepare them by mentioning the road may be a little bumpy at first, but eventually it's going to be a smooth ride—and, hopefully, a lot more fun since it will increase sales!

As the heavy lifting gets underway, be mindful of whether everyone is rewarded fairly and equitably for new roles or tasks the team members take on. It's also important to be mindful of everyone's workload. After all, if you have employees you'd like to hang on to, you don't want to lose them or have them burn out. And w see your sales numbers begin to increase, you may find it he to move the marketing team to an incentive-based bonus sy Consider taking steps to make sure, so far as is possible, that entire process is a positive experience.

Have two kick-off meetings to get the ball rolling. In your first kick-off meeting, the talking points should include:

- Why you are meeting,
- Creating a more cohesive future, and
- Information about top-level buy-in

From there identify key players, make introductions (if necessary), and to make everyone comfortable, invite questions. *Be sure to visit MDM.com/TDDBook to download the Worksheets, Checklists, Agendas, Guidebooks, etc. referred to in this book.* The Agendas we've prepared for you can be customized and used to keep your meetings on track and ensure everyone is on the same page.

After the meeting, try to get a sense of the vibe in the office. If you think the meeting went well, terrific. A day or two later, though, continue being vigilant. Try to assess whether the two teams are happy. Don't be surprised if there is some pushback. If any new issues crop up, add them to your *Barrier Elimination Worksheet* and work through them. If you feel that either group is unhappy, it's best to get to the bottom of their issues and address them before any resulting negativity has a chance to spread.

Stick me on your laptop!

Show the world you're a Digital Distributor!!!

In your second kick-off meeting, which should be held the very next week, your team will have some quick and easy worksheets to complete together that will help them begin to align. The first is the *Inventory of Value-adds Worksheet.* On it the team will list all your value-adds, including every service and solution your company offers that customers would find valuable, whether paid or complimentary. The final product will be a list of all the ways your company provides value to its customers, a brief description of each service and solution, and the benefits each provides to your customers.

By the way, do all your employees know about the various value-adds you offer to your customers and why each is offered? If not, this would be great information to share within your organization.

As you move through this process in the weeks to come, chances are you may think of new services or solutions to add to your offerings in the future. Capture those services on this sheet as well or start a new worksheet for future value-adds. Everyone in your organization should be well-versed on the value-adds you offer.

The next worksheet is the *Customer Experience Worksheet.* On this worksheet, they'll list every touch between your company and your customers. Each of these touches affects your customers' decisions to work with you. From navigating your website to placing an order, from your return process to calls to customer service, from your deliveries to a salesperson's responsiveness — all this and more impacts your customer relationships.

The team will be instructed to list all areas where your customers interact with or are touched by your company. They'll also be asked to describe how customers may generally perceive that experience. Lastly, the instructions will have them list any suggestions for making improvements to that customer experience.

Remember, an outstanding customer experience should be your overall goal. Recognizing and examining every point of customer contact will help expose any wrinkles in your systems and allow everyone in the organization to consistently deliver excellent customer service.

The two worksheets mentioned above work well from a discovery standpoint to identify knowledge about your customers and your customers' experiences from both your sales team's point of view as well as that of your marketing team. *Completing the worksheets together will work as a powerful ice breaker*, and it will be a worthwhile learning experience for both teams about the operations and thought processes of the other, and most importantly, about your customers.

As your project progresses, the teams will generate even more information to help them complete and/or modify the two worksheets. As will be true for most of the worksheets presented throughout the book, they will act as tools to be used and referred to throughout the project and the life of the organization.

An Overview of What Comes Next

Once the project has officially kicked off and the ice has been broken, plan to have your teams continue their alignment by progressing through the meetings listed below.

Meetings 1–3: The Buyer Persona Creation Process

The first order at hand for the two teams is to create your buyer personas (often referred to as avatars). Plan to have at least two or three (or possibly more) meetings to get the *Buyer Persona Worksheets* completed.

The completion of the *Buyer Persona Worksheets* will be a real eye-opener for everyone who participates. There is always an enormous amount of discovery that takes place during this process. It is painstaking and at times can be quite challenging, but it's an effective way to continue breaking down any walls that still may exist between the two teams, and it will add tremendous value to your business.

As the teams complete the buyer persona process, they will segment your audience and then recognize and capture the goals, challenges, and obstacles each of your customer segments face; and I guarantee they will identify information so vital to understanding your customers that everyone will wish you had completed the buyer personas years ago. In Chapter Two, you will find everything you need for this exercise.

Meetings 4 and 5: The Content-Mapping Process

Once your buyer personas have been completed, the next step will be to map your content. Again, both teams will be involved.

Content mapping is a process in which you identify the content to create around each buyer persona's pain points or goals at each stage in their buyer's journey. This process ensures your company is communicating the right information to the right audience at the time it's most significant to them.

Content mapping can be as difficult as creating the buyer personas, and it's important that everyone participates and provides input. The teams will work on, agree on, and understand 1) what content to create and 2) when the content gets shared with each customer segment and why.

For example, testimonials and case studies are considered content, so they will be added to the list of content to be created. The content-mapping process will direct you on how to plan or map where, how, and when buyers should see testimonials during the sales cycle vs. when they should be presented with case studies. We will cover content mapping in depth in Chapter Three.

Besides showing how and when to deploy various content pieces, the content-mapping process will also identify deficits in your content library. Perhaps, your company doesn't have any case studies or testimonials prepared. In such a situation, the marketing and sales teams would work together to create them.

Upon reaching the point in time where your content mapping is in progress, the value of aligning the sales and marketing teams will begin to become clearer to everyone involved. The teams will have become more comfortable working together because everyone will understand the endpoint at which the project is aiming.

Meetings 6 and 7: Choosing a Marketing Automation System

Once you know the kind of content you would like to generate and share with your audience, it's time to start exploring marketing automation systems. Before choosing a system, however, the teams should discuss what they would like to accomplish. You may already have marketing automation or a similar system that you would like to keep for the time being. For example, Constant Contact or MailChimp may be what you use, and either of those may suffice for now.

Still, the teams should take some time to explore various marketing automation platforms, note their features, and decide what they'd like to have vs. what they need, and when they'd like to add new features. They should discuss budget issues and contracts and determine who will be responsible for maintaining the system. Will it be your inside sales team or your marketing team? Or perhaps it should be IT's responsibility to maintain. For this series of meetings, it is important to have an IT rep participate.

As your digital sales and marketing endeavors grow, so will your need for a more robust platform. We'll cover more about marketing automation and technology in Chapter Four, where you will be provided with comparison tools, checklists, and some helpful literature to guide you.

Meetings 8–10: Lead Scoring

After your marketing automation is in place, the next topic to discuss will be lead scoring. Lead scoring is the practice of assigning a score to a prospect based on the prospect's title, ability to make or influence buying decisions, what the prospect has shown interest in along with other buying signals, and where he is in the sales funnel. A lead score will be an important measurement in determining when an MQL (marketing-qualified lead) becomes an SQL (sales-qualified lead) and gets passed over to sales to pursue and close. Lead scoring will help your salespeople focus on the high-value leads generated through your digital efforts, while the weaker leads continue to be nurtured.

Most distributors as of this writing believe that leads generated through the internet come from two places: 1) from their eCommerce site, or 2) from someone subscribing to their newsletter. However, the leads that come from your eCommerce site are NOT leads, they are customers and should be treated as such (see the fourth quadrant in the graphic of the sales cycle shared earlier in this chapter). And the leads generated from someone subscribing to your newsletter may also be customers or, at best, they have not been qualified and will not be eligible for a sales rep's valuable time until they've been further developed.

Right now, many distributors' leads almost always get passed directly to sales. Remember our example of the gym equipment distributor earlier? Your salespeople's time is too valuable to spend on leads generated either by subscribing to your newsletter or through an online sale. Neither have indicated any interest in making a purchase or an additional purchase. At least not yet.

Instead, to avoid wasting your salesperson's time, these leads can be placed in an automated nurturing sequence, which will help determine where their interests lie. Once a lead is in a nurturing sequence, the salesperson (actually your marketing automation system and CRM) will have collected valuable information about the lead, and your salesperson could follow along as the lead moves from cold to warm.

In the lead-scoring series of meetings, you will also start planning workflows, deciding on the path your prospects should take through your sales funnels. These workflows will be based on a lead's actions, demographics, and/or behavior. The workflows will also include determining which notifications about each lead captured will go to your salespeople. (How this works will become clearer in Chapter Four.)

For example, will your salespeople want to know when a prospect downloads an eBook about a particular product line or solution? Will the sales team be interested in whether the prospect clicked to read an article or sat through your webinar? These and other trackable behaviors and actions should be discussed when meeting about lead scoring and workflows. Chapter Five will provide you with the information and tools that take you through the lead scoring process and the activities involved in creating an effective and successful lead capture / follow-up system.

Meeting 11: Setting Your KPIs (Key Performance Indicators)

At this point, everyone should have a clear idea of the types of KPIs they'd like to see from your digital sales and marketing campaigns. This is when you'll begin setting some measurable goals. You'll start by setting a baseline to measure against. Then, the team will decide what you collectively believe constitutes a successful campaign. Will it be ten new leads per month? Twenty? Fifty? Will you expect to see an increase in sales volume? By how much? Eventually, you will also predict the length of the average sales cycle and then measure and adjust based on how close to the mark each sale occurs.

After deciding on an appropriate amount of time to test what has been created, you'll begin measuring. You'll examine whether you've hit your KPIs and adjust accordingly. You'll also identify what the teams could have done better, what worked and what did not, and what changes, if any, will help improve performance. You might also brainstorm with the teams to identify new ideas to test out.

This meeting, by the way, doesn't have to take place immediately following the previous one. You may prefer to wait until your plans are in place and your strategies have been built, tested, and are running well so that the data you measure will be reliable. In Chapter Six, you will find what you need to proceed with measuring your data successfully.

What to Expect Once You're Up and Running

As your new digital sales and marketing processes begin coming together, consider the various team issues that may develop, including issues around each member's performance.

Are the right people being tasked with the work? Is the team working cohesively? Is everyone being compensated fairly and equitably based on the value they bring to the process? These are just a few of the issues that may come up.

Be sure to consider employee-retention issues and salary issues. Is everyone on the team happy in their new role? Are employees working longer hours? Is the work more challenging? If so, should your organization increase team members' compensation or introduce an incentive plan? Conversely, is there someone who isn't working out? If so, why? In writing this, a distributor who almost lost their Marketing Director for similar reasons comes to mind:

This Marketing Director was proactive and very effective when it came to rebate programs. He also acquired tens of thousands of dollars in co-op money for the advertising budget. He and his team handled all the signage and digital displays in their 100+ branches. They had well-attended customer events all summer long, and it's probably not an exaggeration to say the VP of Sales and Marketing couldn't run the marketing function without him. The Director was their shining star.

Then the company recognized the need to put a digital sales and marketing strategy in place.

They explored a few different software possibilities and eventually purchased some robust marketing automation and CRM technology. The marketing team members assured the Director and the VP that they could quickly get a handle on the software. Everyone involved in the decision to purchase the software had high hopes and expectations.

The software package came with a thirty-day set-up and training period, sufficient to get the tech-savvy marketing team up and running with the software. Everything went very well during those thirty days. The marketing team was trained on the software's key aspects, and the team members assured the Director and others involved with the project that they were learning everything necessary to move forward.

However, once the thirty days ran out, the marketing team quickly found themselves in over their heads. The trainers at the software company made it look easier to manage than it was, and over the next few months, the marketing team that had once run like a well-oiled machine was stressed out, angry, and at each other's throats. The Marketing Director was put in a precarious situation because of this. He hadn't learned the software himself, nor did he have room on his plate to take it on.

He and the VP of Sales and Marketing had to determine how best to handle the situation. They had a lot of decisions to think through.

Should the new software and the building of the marketing campaigns fall on the Marketing Director's shoulders? If so, to what extent?

Should he also be responsible for executing the campaigns? If not, then who?

Should the company replace the existing marketing team with a team more skilled in this type of technology?

Or should they increase headcount by bringing in a Sales Assistant or additional marketing team member to run the software's nuts-and-bolts?

What would you do in their position?

All the stories in this book, by the way, are relatively commonplace. I share them with you because they describe situations that can easily happen with any distributor. My hope is that these stories will help prepare you for what may crop up in your organization.

Using competitive digital sales and marketing strategies and tactics can put your business way ahead of the rest of your market, but you'll likely see these new strategies result in a significant paradigm shift that many will find uncomfortable.

In other words, it's going to be foreign at first for most involved. Nonetheless, it's fair to say that it's crucial to your business that you build your foundation correctly and prepare for things to occasionally go sideways. After all, if you stick with comfortable, you're not ever going to grow, and your company will miss out on what could have been a strong future.

While we're on the subject of discomfort, here's another thought to consider and prepare for. Once your new systems are up and running, you may (or eventually should) have situations in which you will be able to track the specific activities that led to a sale. Which means you (and the teams involved) will also be able to identify whose work was responsible for converting that sale. You will know how customers found you, what moved them through the sales process, and, quite possibly, what led them to purchase. You and your team will likely know every touchpoint because your marketing automation system will capture it.

Suppose your marketing team played a substantial role in capturing and nurturing that customer. Will your organization compensate the marketing team as it would a salesperson who converted a similar deal? If not, how will the marketing team react?

These are just a few of the issues to be aware of as you move through the processes laid out for you.

If you haven't already done so, visit MDM.com/TDDBook to download the Worksheets, Checklists, Agendas, Guidebooks, etc. referred to in this book.

CHAPTER 2

Creating Your Buyer Personas

"Buyer personas help ensure that all activities involved in acquiring and serving your customers are tailored to the targeted buyer's needs. That may sound like a no-brainer, but it isn't as simple as it sounds. If you really pay attention to the way companies present themselves, you'll begin to notice that many of them start by talking about what they do – not what the customer needs. This puts them at odds with the way people make decisions.

When choosing a product or service, people naturally gravitate toward businesses they know and trust. And the best way to build trust is to show genuine understanding and concern for the other person – in this case, your customers. Gaining trust as a business requires a subtle, but important, shift in the way in which you present yourself. First, show your potential customers that you get them by addressing their pain or need - only then will they be open to exploring what you have to offer."[3]

---

3   Wright, Amy. "What is a Buyer Persona and Why is It Important?" *Social Media Today,* October 17, 2017. https://www.socialmediatoday.com/news/what-is-a-buyer-persona-and-why-is-it-important/507404/. Accessed April 2021.

Creating buyer personas will be one of the most challenging processes you will encounter in this book. Nonetheless, the benefits your company will gain by going through this exercise are worth the effort. In fact, I'm confident that, once you are finished, you will wish you had done this years ago!

Using a buyer persona as a tool to guide your company's communications with each of your audience segments will help you position yourselves as a reliable partner whose sole aim is to serve its customers. So, while creating buyer personas is a challenging exercise, doing so is critical to successfully completing the steps covered in the next four chapters and, even more importantly, it will give you information that is critical to your company's future success.

A buyer persona is a semi-fictional representation of your ideal customer. It's a model your sales and marketing teams create based on their knowledge and experience with your current customers. If, like most companies, your business has multiple audiences it sells to or services, you must create a buyer persona for each audience segment.

Your buyer personas should be captured using the *Buyer Persona Worksheets* provided in the supplemental materials for this book. This is a tool you will use going forward that will give you structure and guidance with creating all your sales and marketing messaging. Once complete, your sales and marketing teams will continue to refine and occasionally refer back to your completed *Buyer Persona Worksheets* in order to stay in touch with, and often ahead of, customers' issues and concerns. These worksheets will be the keeper of the information you will use to match up the valuable services and solutions your business can offer to what best helps each customer segment with their challenges.

If your business has multiple audiences but does not create buyer personas for each segment, your ability to address your audiences' goals, pain points, and struggles will become less precise and much more impersonal. By not using personas when crafting your messaging, your sales and marketing messages will tend to be diluted and less effective.

Today more than ever, customers have come to expect messaging to be more personalized and targeted to their needs. Weaker, untargeted sales and marketing collateral will fall flat.

Your Value Lies in Your Problem-Fixing Abilities

Logically, you would initially believe that most communication from your sales and marketing departments should revolve around your products, their features, and why they should be purchased from you. Up until recently, in fact, this approach worked well for a distributor.

But today, with competition being what it's become, you must consistently, in all communications, make it clear that *your business exists to solve your customers' problems. To remain relevant, you must make your customers aware that you provide the solutions and services your customers need.* It's that simple. If this isn't made clear in your communications, and your communications do not revolve around your customers, your company becomes just another distributor who sells products.

Does this mean you should halt product promotion? No, of course not. But what it does mean is that every communication you put out — including those that promote your products — should emphasize *why* the product is the best choice, or a possible choice, for the individual reading that message.

Now, you may be wondering, "What if an item or product line we're promoting is the best choice for only *some* of my customers?" If that's the case, then that product line should only be promoted to the customer segments that would benefit from the promotion. You've got to get the right message in front of the right person and *only* the right person.

Since the beginning of time, it's been easy for distributors to get the right message in front of the right person — that's why you pay your salespeople so well. But today, in a world where your prospects and customers are bombarded with information from all directions, coupled with the difficulties of making face-to-face sales calls, it's just no longer the case.

For several reasons, the distribution industry has reached what can be a devastating inflection point, but it doesn't have to be devastating at all. You simply need to learn and deploy new strategies to communicate your value. The good news is that you don't have to invent these strategies — many industries before you have already been down this road. So, we already know what works.

In distribution, now, more than ever, your messaging should emphasize your services and solutions in a way that differentiates your company from your competition. In other words, instead of selling products, which anyone can do (and *is* doing it seems), communicate to your audience why working with you is in their best interest… why choosing to work with you vs. a competitor is the best decision they can make. But you've got to communicate in a way that puts the focus on the buyer, not on your company.

Let's look for a minute at how effectively communicating your value, aka your problem-solving abilities, becomes challenging.

You can start by saying that clearly, your company provides a lot of value. If it didn't, you wouldn't be in business. And it's probably not difficult to talk about or write about your value. In other words, communicating the right messaging is easy. Again, it's what your salespeople do for a living.

The difficulty lies in the second part of the challenge — getting the right message *in front of the right person.* Translated, and what's so difficult, is that this also means '*not* getting that message in front of the *wrong* person,' especially if the wrong person is someone whom you might want to communicate with again.

In other words, if you are sending or sharing information to prospects or customers that doesn't apply to them, there's a good chance they will stop reading your communications altogether.

Because of how technology has evolved, people today are conditioned to expect a certain level of personalization. And while that expectation may be almost subliminal, your ability to 'get the message right' will undoubtedly affect a buyer's perception of how well you can serve him.

And so, to understand who your prospects and customers really are, and which message each should get, you've got to segment your audience, which brings us back to the original mission of creating your buyer personas.

The *Buyer Persona Worksheets* we're giving you with this book have been customized specifically for distributors, so they will help you stay focused on bringing actual value to your customers. Value, of course, can take more than one form. Value could be a resource you share, a solution you sell, a discount on a product you know customers want, or any other offer in the form of assistance. For customers to recognize value, it must be presented in a way that speaks directly to them and is explicitly for their benefit.

Whatever the form, it is best to not assume customers will recognize why a given product or solution is valuable to them. Your messaging should make it abundantly clear why what you are offering is explicitly for them. Use clear statements such as: "We are here to help you by offering you X, and this is why X is of value to you"; *or* "By offering you X, we are helping you in a way our competitors cannot. This is how."

The more you know about your customers and which segment you are addressing, the more tailored your messages (and their experience) can be, and the more impact your messages will carry.

Segmenting Your Audience

You will begin creating your buyer personas by capturing as much knowledge as possible about each of your audience segments. Your salespeople will, of course, have the most information to contribute, but other departments that interact with your customers should also be consulted. Then, do some further research to learn more about that audience, including their needs, wants, struggles, and goals.

The buyer personas will ultimately become a depiction of your perfect customers. When finished, all the marketing and sales messaging the team develops will be based on the finished buyer personas. We'll walk through the process in detail below.

You may have created buyer personas in the past, but because customers' needs change over time, it is vital to review your buyer personas every nine months to a year. Doing so will help reinforce the habit of focusing your messaging on the benefits of your services and solutions versus simple product sales.

For example, think back to when COVID-19 first arrived on the scene. Very few distributors knew how or what to communicate, so they continued to do what they had always done — sell products. Many distributors sent reminders to their customers to let them know that although their branches were closed, curb-side pickup was still available. Some customers found messages like this helpful, but others may have found it a bit thoughtless.

The customers who were still in operation appreciated knowing products were available, but the customers who had shut down hoped to hear a message that was more supportive and reassuring. Many were small business owners who suddenly found themselves on the brink of disaster. They needed a lifeline, a role that a product from a distributor's shelves could not play. Eventually, most distributors understood what was weighing on their customers and recognized that COVID-19 was an excellent opportunity to become that lifeline for their customers. But for many, it took a while to really understand how best to serve their customers early on.

The *Buyer Persona Worksheets* created for this book capture information that allows you to segment your customers at a very granular level, digging deep into customer needs. They'll clarify and bring information to light about *how* you can best support your customers. For example, a distributor that had completed their buyer personas before COVID-19 hit could have used the information generated to reveal what customers would be struggling with. The worksheets could also have provided guidance to the distributor in knowing what they could have done to help their customers.

Once your buyer personas are created and regularly consulted, your sales and marketing messaging will tune in directly to your customers' goals, needs, pain points, and even threats to your customers' businesses. As a result, leveraging this information in your messaging shows your customers that your company is in the business of *helping* as opposed to simply selling them products; and your customers' trust and loyalty will strengthen and grow.

Completed *Buyer Persona Worksheets* help to eliminate the blurred lines between customer segments, gray areas that may result in overgeneralizations in your sales and marketing materials. Let's say your company sells to residential builders and commercial builders as well as to small builders and large builders. That's four different segments — small residential, large residential, small commercial, and large commercial.

Your salespeople know the conversations they should have with members of each customer segment, and likely each conversation will be similar with subtle, albeit very important, differences. This is because each segment has similar needs, *and* each has different needs. Because of their experience in the field with your customers, your salespeople will know those similarities and differences, and they will use that knowledge to communicate effectively with each audience. But your marketing team will not be aware of those subtle differences, and they may not see the importance and effectiveness of crafting their marketing pieces to better target your audiences using these distinctions.

The buyer persona creation exercise will capture and document the similarities and differences of each audience. Your marketing team can then incorporate that information into your sales and marketing collateral to better target and resonate with the individuals who see your marketing messages.

In addition to your completed *Buyer Persona Worksheets* being the guiding force behind every piece of content you create, the worksheets are also instrumental in completing the content-mapping process, covered in Chapter Three. The content-mapping process dictates the topics and formats of the content to be generated and is instrumental in deciding how your company will promote your materials, where you will promote them, and when to promote each piece of content.

A priceless benefit of the buyer persona creation process is that it will allow your salespeople to share their knowledge about your customers with your marketing team and the rest of your employees. Executives often assume their employees know their customers well, but, based on my experience, this is not always the case. There is information your salespeople know that will help shape your sales and marketing collateral so that it contains more powerful messaging. The information your salespeople share may also help shape how the rest of your organization serves your customers. These insights should be captured on the *Buyer Persona Worksheet* and shared with employees so that everyone better understands and serves your customers.

Product services, marketing, customer service, and perhaps other teams as well contribute to the overall customer experience your company delivers. The more the people on your client-facing teams know about your customers, the better equipped they are to serve your customers, and the better the customers' experiences will be. Actionable knowledge about your customers begins with the information you are sure to uncover by completing *Buyer Persona Worksheets*.

As critical as the worksheets are to your sales and marketing processes, it's important to remember that buyer personas are not foolproof. The information the completed worksheets contain is based on real people, and people change. *It is important that you continue to treat your customers and prospects like persons, not personas.* In other words, regardless of what the worksheet tells you, always trust your gut and use common sense.

An example would be, once again, when COVID-19 hit. Some distributors treated their customers as though it were business as usual despite their customers' needs having changed almost overnight. Other distributors immediately recognized the shift in customers' needs and changed their communications to focus on COVID-related issues instead.

The Process of Creating Buyer Personas

In a few minutes, you are going to go through the exercise of how an electrical supplies distributor would complete a *Buyer Persona Worksheet*. Before you get started, below is a rough outline of the information we normally collect and analyze about each buyer persona.

- The persona's demographics
    - » Gender, age, income
    - » Personality and style (friendly, impulsive, calm, aggressive)
    - » Communication preferences (email, calls via cell or office, text messaging)
- Their top three to five goals, struggles, and/or pain points
- Their challenges with each goal, struggle, and/or pain point
- The ways your organization could help them achieve their goals or challenges or relieve their pain points
- The obstacles your buyer persona faces with each
- How your organization can help them overcome these obstacles
- The top three to five reasons why the persona would want to engage your services
- The objections you hear most often

Now let's look at a handful of buyer personas representing customers who might purchase from our fictitious electrical supplies distributor. Their customers would most likely include:

- Large residential electrical contractors
- Small residential electrical contractors
- Large commercial electrical contractors
- Small commercial electrical contractors
- OEMs (original equipment manufacturers)
- Educational facilities (universities or school districts)
- Healthcare facilities

When you have multiple customer segments, your first inclination may be to create messaging that speaks to all or many customer segments at once. For example, everyone on the list above purchases lighting, switches, and wire; but we also know each segment is buying these products for somewhat different reasons. And because the above list of personas can be somewhat overwhelming, our electrical distributor's first inclination might be to market lighting, switches, and wire generically, without focusing on any one group's goals, challenges, or pain points. This way, the distributor's marketing materials will focus on the general features of the products because, by focusing on the features of the products, the same messaging can be used for all the audience segments. Doing so sounds efficient, but it's not.

Homogenizing the messaging is not effective in catching someone's attention. Although the segments mentioned above purchase many of the same products, each has slightly different goals or pain points to resolve, which equates to each having slightly different reasons for buying.

A healthcare facility will be interested in certain aspects of a lighting product that may not appeal to a small residential contractor. And what appeals to a large residential contractor may not appeal to a healthcare facility or even the small residential contractor. What often happens is, instead of reaching everyone, sales and marketing messages that are generic and features-based will connect with no one because the messages are not targeted or relatable to anyone.

Buyer personas help identify the differences that matter to your audiences quickly and easily and allow you to focus on those differences to *enhance* or *strengthen* your sales and marketing messages.

In upcoming examples you will see that since each persona equate to a significant chunk of business, our electrical distributor will sell their products using similar yet different messaging for each segment. While doing so means the distributor will have a separate message for each of the seven groups, it also m have much better chances of selling more products and bu stronger relationships with their customers. Moreover, with dynamic technology, *this is not difficult to do!*

Deciding Where to Start

There is a lot of work involved in creating each buyer persona, so it is probably best to complete just a few personas at a time to avoid getting bogged down. Which should you work on first? I would suggest starting with the customer segment(s) your business wants more of. It could be the customer segments that purchase the highest volume, or it might be your most profitable customers. Then again you might choose the customers you are most comfortable working with.

Stick me on your laptop! Show the world you're a Digital Distributor!!!

To get your feet wet, consider focusing on personas for whom the *Buyer Persona Worksheet* is the easiest to complete—your most common buyers, those who require the least amount of research, you attract the highest volume of, or are the easiest to draw in. Focus on completing one buyer persona at a time and, for planning purposes, remember the process can be a time-intensive exercise.

Let's Put This to Work

Below are examples of two buyer personas that an electrical supplies distributor would create. We'll use them to illustrate the process. Think of your own business and your own customers as you follow along.

The first is a buyer persona for a small residential electrical contractor and the other is for a large commercial electrical contractor. By comparing the two, my hope is that by seeing the similarities and differences in the two, you'll have a running start in creating your own personas.

As you do, you'll find over time that the buyer persona process gets easier as you get more granular. The more granular the information you capture, the more focused and targeted your collateral will be.

Your target audience (i.e., your buyer persona) will usually be the key decision-maker in the segment you are targeting, and the decision-maker isn't always the owner. The small residential contractor is the decision-maker and owner of the business. For the large commercial contractor, however, the decision-maker is a buyer, an employee.

Demographics:	
Small Electrical Contractor	**Large Electrical Contractor**
<ul><li>Male, aged 35-65.</li><li>Usually a blue-collar worker who eventually branched out and opened his own business.</li><li>Married with kids; family-oriented but always busy with a lot on his mind.</li><li>Works hard, is cost conscious, owns his own home.</li><li>Income is probably $60,000 to $80,000 a year—maybe $100,000, depending on location.</li><li>Self-disciplined, focused on work, customer centric.</li><li>Work often overlaps with personal time.</li><li>Essentially the sole decision-maker for the business; often consults his wife on business decisions.</li><li>Communication preference would be digital (email or text message). He is usually the guy who is doing the work, so he often does not answer the phone.</li><li>Cost conscious and value conscious, this person is very hands-on and is keenly aware of every dollar that goes in and out of the business.</li></ul>	<ul><li>Male, sometimes female, aged 28 to 65.</li><li>They may have started as a blue-collar worker or may be college-educated. Works in a corporate / office environment. This person's title is Purchasing Agent or Buyer.</li><li>There is a good chance they have a business/corporate background in addition to their knowledge of electrical supplies.</li><li>Married or single, may or may not have children, may or may not be family oriented.</li><li>Their income will come in at around $60,000 to $65,000, maybe more depending on the area and years in the business.</li><li>Day ends at 5 pm and work does not mix with personal life.</li><li>Decision-making may be more of a collective process and would possibly include, in addition to the Buyer, some combination of a Superintendent, a Project Manager, and a Foreman. They might all have some influence in the decision-making process.</li><li>Prefers to communicate via office phone or cellphone.</li><li>In choosing product, it's quite possible this person puts time ahead of cost. They may be willing to spend more money to keep a job on schedule. They bid on jobs that are in the millions of dollars, so they may be willing to spend extra money to keep their jobs moving forward.</li></ul>

When it comes to recognizing the goals of each of the two personas, hold off on tying their goals to your products and services just yet. Rather, *put your products and your services to the side, and try to get inside the heads of your buyers to understand what motivates them.*

Top 3-5 Goals:	
Small Electrical Contractor	**Large Electrical Contractor**
• To build a successful business that provides for his family. • To provide value to his customers, maintain strong relationships with them, and get referrals from them. • To manage his time and his workers' time efficiently and productively. • To eventually sell his business. • To stay up to date with code as well as new technologies.	• To stay within time and bid constraints. • To keep everyone on the job happy and moving forward. • To procure cutting-edge, top-of-the-line products at a reasonable price. • To have access to a wide selection of products. • To keep his or her job.

Let's talk about the *challenges* that the two personas have. You might find that the challenges seem analogous to the goals. The buyer persona process is designed to ask for the same information in various ways to tease out more specific, detailed, and well-rounded answers.

Top 3-5 Challenges:	
Small Electrical Contractor	**Large Electrical Contractor**
• Finding good employees who stick around. • Keeping up with technology. • Finding new customers/building his business. • Balancing inventory and cost. • Time management.	• Finding suppliers they can trust and rely on. • Keeping up with technology. • Balancing cost and quality. • Keeping upper management happy by keeping the job moving forward. • Time management.

Notice that there are similarities between the two personas, but when you dig into them, you'll see the similarities are just that — similar. The technology the small contractor uses will likely be different than the technology the buyer at the large contractor uses. Time management equates to something very different to the two as well.

In the next step of the buyer persona process, our distributor chooses which goal or challenge it can help the buyer persona with, stating why they chose it, and explaining what they can do to help the persona achieve the goal or overcome the challenge.

Below, on behalf of our fictitious electrical distributor, we chose one goal for each of our personas.

Small Electrical Contractor:

Goal #1:
To build a successful, small business that provides for his family.

Why we chose this goal:
We want him to be successful almost as much as he does. It's good for our company to help keep him successful because it will strengthen our relationship with him, build trust, and hopefully we will become his distributor of choice.

What we can do to help them achieve this goal:
We can create and provide a survey that identifies any weaknesses or trouble spots in this buyer persona's business so that we can know exactly what they need.

We can then provide an educational series that teaches this persona how to improve in the areas identified.

We could also create a mentor/mentee program in which our more seasoned employees with certain business or industry knowledge (probably sales reps) act as mentors by sharing knowledge that helps this persona with his business.

Large Electrical Contractor (Buyer):

Goal #1:

To stay within time and bid constraints. To not allow the project to eat into the bottom line.

Why we chose this goal:

If we can help the persona achieve this goal, then he looks good to his management and his team. And if we help him look good and take some of the pressure off him, he's going to remember and do business with us again. We become more than just another distributor he happened to buy product from.

What we can do to help the persona achieve this goal:

We can follow up with the persona more frequently. We can check in with our manufacturers to see whether any troubleshooting is necessary in procuring product.

We can continuously monitor the progress of the project.

We can give the persona a dedicated internal resource and a VIP-level of customer service *(which directly connects to the customer experience issue mentioned above).*

Now that we've identified a goal (or challenge) to focus in on and help assist our personas with, the next step is to identify a key obstacle or obstacles the persona would have in achieving that goal (or overcoming that challenge), and then describe what the distributor can do to help overcome the obstacle. Then, our distributor would identify the benefits they provide in helping the persona overcome the obstacle.

Small Electrical Contractor:

In terms of the first goal or challenge, what is a key obstacle the persona is facing?

Building a successful business that supports his family is a struggle that never seems to end. He knows very little about business, and finds that the more he learns, the more he realizes he doesn't know much about the business end of things.

What can we do to help him overcome this obstacle?

We can provide educational video training that he can watch on his own time. We also can create a Q&A business hotline where he can reach us for help or advice.

What benefits could we provide?

The most important thing to this persona's business is that he provides value to his customers. If he doesn't, he will lose customers, could lose his business, and we could lose business as a result. We can provide him with the benefit of allowing him to serve his customers better. Benefits can be in the form of education, as mentioned earlier, favorable credit terms, flexible pricing programs, flexible delivery schedules or will-call services, and offering him less costly product lines.

Large Electrical Contractor:

In terms of the first goal or challenge, what is a key obstacle the persona is facing?

The goal we identified for the large electrical contractor was to stay within time and budget constraints. An obstacle would be that on a big project there are many different variables that need to be managed to keep the job within the scope of service, under or at budget, or with an early or on-time completion. It's a lot for anyone to manage.

What can we do to help the large electrical contractor overcome this obstacle?

Chances are, whatever issues this customer runs into, we've seen them before, so we can forewarn the buyer of potential pitfalls. We can share firsthand examples of how other large electrical contractors handled situations he may find himself in. And if the buyer needs additional resources, perhaps we can point them in the direction of those resources.

What benefits could we provide?

It's a tremendous benefit to the buyer to have someone in his corner who "knows the ropes."

By taking an interest in his success, we're giving him the benefit of our knowledge and access to resources he may not be aware of. We can take on the role of a confidante or informal advisor, which will strengthen our relationship with him for years to come.

You would then repeat the process of choosing the next goal or challenge to work on for the persona, identifying why you chose that goal or challenge, what obstacles he may encounter that you can help him overcome, and what benefits you're bringing him by helping him.

Hopefully, by reading through the differences in the various ways an electrical distributor can support both large and small contractors, some ideas were sparked about your own business and how your company can help your customers work through their challenges and reach their goals.

Now, let's shift gears and look inward at our electrical supplies distributor's business. This next section is where the distributor identifies the top three to five reasons the buyer personas would want to work with them. Note that both columns below are identical. This is because we would be hard-pressed to find any distributor who *didn't* list the five items below as their response. For this reason, *distributors must show they are willing to go beyond the reasons listed below if they want to differentiate themselves and become the distributor of choice.*

3-5 Reasons Why They'd Want to Engage Your Services:	
Small Electrical Contractor	**Large Electrical Contractor**
• Our industry knowledge and longevity in the business.	• Our industry knowledge and longevity in the business.
• Our expansive inventory and delivery capabilities.	• Our expansive inventory and delivery capabilities.
• Our generous credit terms.	• Our generous credit terms.
• Our willingness to help provide one-off solutions to customer issues.	• Our willingness to help provide one-off solutions to customer issues.
• Our position as a consultative partner versus just a company that sells products.	• Our position as a consultative partner versus just a company that sells products.

The next two sections of the worksheet are company-specific, so I will leave it to you to fill in these sections on your own. The first section asks you to identify the common objections your salespeople hear most often, either related to the goals and challenges you have listed on the sheet or related to any other issues.

You'll capture the objections on this form because, once identified, your marketing team can address customer objections in the marketing collateral they produce. By doing so, your collateral will continue to move your customers and prospects through the sales funnel more smoothly. This is not a step to miss.

The last section of the *Buyer Persona Worksheet* asks how you would describe your solution to the persona. Here is where you will capture your value proposition. Does your company have one? If not, perhaps it's time to start developing one. A value proposition tells people why they should do business with you. It should be worded in a way that convinces people that doing business with your organization is a far superior choice than doing business with your competitors. If you don't already have a pre-written value proposition, consider working on it in this step, but keep in mind that writing a value proposition usually requires some wordsmithing, and so writing a value proposition that covers your entire company might be a work in progress for a while.

An alternative, in the meantime, is to write value propositions specifically for the various solutions you offer, similar to what you've done with your *Buyer Persona Worksheet*, but with the focus specifically on the solution itself (vs. the buyer persona).

To do this use the *Solutions Promotion Worksheet* and combine the information from your *Inventory of Value-adds Worksheet* with your *Buyer Persona Worksheets*. You would work on the *Solutions Promotion Worksheet* after you go through the buyer persona process.

The *Solutions Promotion Worksheet* will take the information you have identified in the *Inventory of Value-adds Worksheet* and add the challenges, pain points, goals, or struggles each solution is meant to target for each of your buyer personas. Like the *Buyer Persona Worksheet*, you will also identify why customers would choose your company for each service or solution.

Use the *Solutions Promotion Worksheet* when your marketing team wants to promote a specific solution so that it resonates with various targeted audiences. It will help them determine which segment gets which message about that solution and why.

In Chapter One I mentioned that many people in your company can contribute to the *Buyer Persona Worksheets*. It may be helpful to print the worksheets and share them with other employees to weigh in on as well; then have them gathered back up and summarized. Consider sharing the finished versions of each persona with each employee in your organization for easy reference.

Upon completion, take a few minutes to review, revise and, if necessary, update your *Solutions Promotion Worksheet*, your *Inventory of Value-adds Worksheet*, and perhaps even your *Customer Experience Worksheet* and add any new knowledge that has been uncovered during the buyer persona creation exercise. In Chapter Three, you will apply much of what's been discovered.

Visit MDM.com/TDDBook to download the Worksheets, Checklists, Agendas, Guidebooks, etc. referred to in this book.

CHAPTER 3

Communicating Your Message Digitally

"With trade shows and conferences canceled due to the COVID-19 global pandemic, we see crystal clear why B2B content marketing is important. If you relied on pressing the flesh, it's time to reassess. B2Bs that managed to sit the content marketing revolution out by overcompensating with aggressive direct sales tactics have found themselves between a rock and a hard place.

With almost all business being transacted virtually these days, digital marketing is now the only viable way of finding and pitching qualified leads."[4]

Content marketing has probably been the most frequently mentioned phrase in digital marketing ever. It is collectively the most effective and instrumental strategy an organization can employ to communicate to an audience.

---

4   Schwartzman, Eric. "2021 Guide to B2B Content Marketing." EricSchwartzman.com. https://www.ericschwartzman.com/why-b2b-content-marketing-is-important. Accessed April 2021.

From an About Us page to product descriptions and every word and image in between, businesses depend on the internet to share information that communicates their message and their value. These businesses post information on their websites and on other places on the internet to leverage a search engine's ability to deliver the best possible results to its users.

Search engines are smart and competitive. They generate a tremendous amount of income for their stockholders, as you are no doubt aware, so to maintain their status as the search engine of choice, each search engine company will do all it can to deliver the information its users believe is most valuable.

Content marketing and SEO are two separate marketing strategies that work together to ensure a user gets the best results from their search. Google, of course, has mastered the art of integrating search and content. Google will comb through every word and every bit of data from videos, audios, PDFs, images, and any other media published online to deliver the most accurate and useful results to its users.

People use search engines to find solutions, get their questions answered, and learn new information. For this reason, and I cannot stress this enough, it is a best practice for businesses to create and publish content that is a solution to a problem, answers a question, or educates with information customers look for.

In fact, you may have noticed that if you start a search with the words "How to…" or a similar phrase that asks a question, Google will now feature what it deems to be the 'best answer in a box at the top of page one that also contains a link to the source. It's called the Google Answer Box. It's also referred to as Position 0 on the search engine results pages (SERPs). Having your content appear in the Google Answer Box is an enviable accomplishment because it means your brand has rocketed to the top of the SERPs with minimal effort.

There is a science to appearing in the Google Answer Box, and it's a goal you should reach for as you plan your content. The results found in the Google Answer Box can garner the highest number of clicks and the most traffic. As you would with any science or process-related task, take some time to research what search-engine experts are saying will work to get your brand into the Google Answer Box. <u>Be sure to find research that is relatively recent</u> because technology, especially search-engine algorithms, evolve over time and can become quickly outdated.

The Real Reason Companies Create Content

Creating useful content requires effort, but it is an effort worth making. The more robust your content is, the better its chance of success in the search engines. And the greater the amount of robust marketing pieces you produce, the more opportunities you create for people to discover your company and see it as a resource they can trust.

A company that shares content that its audience is looking for sends the message that they are in the "helping business" rather than merely trying to sell products. The message conveyed to their audiences is that they are an organization that cares about its customers' success. They are showing that it has invested in providing information that either offers a solution to its customers' problems or helps its audiences meet their goals, or both.

Publishing informative, entertaining, and educational content for anyone to read for free creates a perception of selflessness. It shows that the company is willing to share valuable information that helps others while asking for nothing in return. It also demonstrates a company's knowledge and expertise, which will establish them as a leader or expert in their industry. Companies who do this well will attest to it being an excellent way to stand out from competitors.

What is Content Marketing?

Content marketing is a form of marketing that uses content to attract a targeted audience, usually online. Content is any piece of media that has been written or produced for others to consume. Some examples of the more popular forms of content used for digital sales and marketing strategies include:

- Email
- Web Pages
- Blog Posts
- Videos
- Special Reports
- eBooks
- Podcasts
- Infographics

- Slide Decks
- Checklists
- Educational Material
- Social Media Posts
- Case Studies
- Testimonials
- Whitepapers

The list goes on.

The overall goal of content marketing is to 1) get the right content 2) to the right people 3) at the right time 4) in the right format. It's easy to create content that hits one or two of those four points. When you hit three, you are doing a commendable job. The goal, though, is to hit all four because when you do, the chance that the people consuming it will turn into leads is very high.

One of the most popular ways of hitting all four points is to use a technique known as *inbound marketing*. Inbound marketing is the practice of creating and publishing—usually to one's website—content that attracts viewers like a magnet. This content, produced to attract clicks and views, is often referred to as a lead magnet. Digital sales and marketing pros will put a lot of effort into inbound and content marketing because of how effective it can be in attracting customers and new leads.

One-Up Your Competition When Selling Online

I see a high amount of the content published on distributors' websites coming directly from the manufacturers. As a result, distributors who sell the same products publish identical content to their websites. Hopefully, you've taken steps to add additional content to your product descriptions because sharing identical content without additional information added is not a good practice if you want to generate attention. Here's why:

Think of any product your company currently sells online. Now think of the results that appear when someone searches online for that product by name. In all likelihood, the results will be a handful of ads at the very top of page one. Then, below the ads, will be the same (manufacturer's) product image again and again with the same description accompanying it. If the SERPs (search engine results pages) show ten sites with basically the same information, which result will a reader choose?

To stand apart from your competitors, consider doing things differently. Otherwise, you run the risk of being overlooked or unrecognizable on the SERPs, and customers may purchase from a competitor rather than from you.

You may struggle at first to generate new ways to write about your products because many products will not lend themselves to content that makes them stand out or look different. But don't lose hope — there are still some easy content ideas you can try, several of which are very easy and cost-effective.

One best practice is to publish more about your products' benefits (vs. features). Remember from Chapter Two – different benefits for different audiences. Include all the information you can to reach each audience. Another best practice would be to show how a product provides a solution to a problem. Another still would be to simply publish content that competitors would not take the time to do.

Here's a powerful scenario that illustrates this point. Suppose you are an industrial supplier, and like thousands of other industrial suppliers, you sell lap joint flanges—a somewhat boring product with a limited description. Lap joint flanges are sold online by distributors everywhere. They are also being sold on Amazon. Nevertheless, there are several strategies that *may* help ensure customers buy lap joint flanges from you and not your competition.

Here are a few:

- You can employ the best salespeople hoping they'll generate above average sales numbers
- You can go after businesses that purchase the highest volumes of lap joint flanges and give them some extra attention in the hopes they'll give you some extra orders
- You can offer the most competitive pricing
- You can have the best advertising online or in trade magazines

These are all reasonably good suggestions, several of which you may even have tried. The problem is that while you are putting these strategies in place, your competitors are likely doing something similar. Your competitors may employ the best salespeople, who may also pursue the same customers just as vigorously. Your competitors may compete on price, too. And lastly, if you were to invest in advertising, not only is it expensive, but also, what could you advertise about lap joint flanges that would get noticed and make it worth the investment?

Here are two strategies I have found that can differentiate your business from your competition and stand out in a crowded space. The first is one of my favorites: *bundling*. Bundling products gives you the ability to sell stock that may otherwise sit by packaging it with other, more popular products. Bundling also helps increase your average order value.

You could bundle the lap joint flanges with other products and then promote the bundle. When you create a bundle that no one else offers, it will appear differently in the search engines so it will stand out from the competitors. If you're selling on Amazon, it will appear differently there as well. Unique bundles on Amazon also enjoy the benefit of having their own buy box, eliminating any competition for a similar array of products.

Further, product bundles can be easier to market. Leverage holidays and other events to promote your bundles. Featuring your product bundles in your social media strategy can give your products more exposure and new attention. You may even consider promoting a different bundle each month or so. Remember that the two biggest reasons buyers will purchase your bundles are 1) to save money and 2) for convenience. For that reason, be sure your bundles are well thought out and beneficial to your buyers.

Bundling does, however, require a relatively high level of behind-the-scenes manpower. While it's a creative and thoughtful strategy, it can warrant extra time, attention, and effort. You may sell more flanges by bundling, but it may or may not be cost-effective in the long run. Moreover, your competitors may create a similar or more competitive bundle, eventually putting you back at square one.

Is bundling the right sales and marketing strategy for your organization? Perhaps. To help you explore the value of bundling, we've created a *Bundle Creation Worksheet*, which you'll find in your supplemental materials. Use this worksheet to help boost sales and clear your shelves of stagnant products.

The second strategy, which makes more economic sense and delivers a much longer-lasting impact, is *content marketing*. When done correctly, content marketing can save your company a lot of money, and it will help generate many new sales. Here is an example of content marketing at work:

A small, Texas-based industrial supply company sits at the top of page one when someone does a search on "purchase lap joint flange" on Google. As of this writing, the results on Google's page one are as follows: At the very top of the page are paid ads, as is always the case. Then, below the ads, Grainger appears. And then under Grainger is the distributor from Texas. Interestingly, next, under the Texas distributor in third place, is Amazon.

While the exact order of the results will change ever so slightly from day to day, the overall results – with the Texas-based supplier being in the top three – have been consistent for years.

How?!

The ads come up first because the companies that run the ads pay to appear there. If the companies continue to pay Google each month, their ads will continue to appear at the top of the page. If they stop paying Google, they will no longer appear. By the way, at the time of this writing, it costs almost $4.00 per click to have the top spot in the paid ads on Google for 'lap joint flange.'

I believe Grainger comes up first in the SERPs because Grainger gets the most traffic for lap joint flange searches. Google recognizes that Grainger is often the first link clicked and, because Google wants to give people what they believe people are looking for, Google will keep that result at the top, where it is easy to spot. If people keep clicking the Grainger link, Grainger will stay glued to the first position. And if the Grainger link is in the top spot, it will probably continue to be clicked. It's a nice situation to be in.

The small Texas-based distributor appears second, however, for a different reason. It's because of their content marketing strategy for this product. Their website contains a video about lap joint flanges along with a transcription of the video's dialogue. The video isn't very engaging or flashy, but it does provide some instructive information about lap joint flanges. Here is the exact transcription that appears on the page beneath the video:

> *"This is a lap joint flange. The difference between a lap joint flange and a slip-on flange, I want to show you a slip-on flange, which looks very similar. From the outside, it almost looks like the same. But you look on the backside, it has a little radius and a little end right here. Some people confuse it that this is a flat faced flange. It is not.*
>
> *If you look at the difference, if you just look at the backside, you will see that this is different because it has a little radius. I'll show you right now why it has a little radius, that lap joint flange. For example, I have the same flange in stainless steel, this is a stainless steel 304 flange. Whenever you're using a lap joint flange, you use a stub end. The radius is for the stub end, so you do like this and that's why it's called a lap joint flange. You need to have a stub end and that is the purpose of that little radius right there."[5]*

As you can tell from the transcript, their video is straightforward. About two minutes long, it shows a man picking up, holding, and

---

5 "Lap Joint Flanges." *Trupply, LLC.* www.trupply.com/pages/lap-joint-flanges. May 14, 2016. Accessed April 2021.

putting down the various flanges he discusses. The distributor posted it on YouTube, and then from YouTube, the distributor embedded it into their website. It isn't very polished. Anyone with a smartphone and the willingness to share some knowledge could have made the video.

Here's what I think is very exciting for distributors to understand:

- First, a small distributor is at the top of the search engines for this product, appearing between Grainger and Amazon. By the way, the Amazon link leads to where this same distributor has listed his products on Amazon.

- Second, the video, which the distributor posted about five years ago, will remain on the first page of Google for a long time to come without their ever paying a cent to Google or doing anything more with that video. My guess would be that unless the distributor removes it from their website or from YouTube, it will sit on page 1 on Google for many, many more years.

- Third, it is an amazingly simple strategy that any distributor can do!

Does your company spend money to advertise its products and services on Google and other mediums? Do you ever wonder how much of that could be saved by launching a content marketing campaign instead? The most significant difference between an ad campaign and a content marketing campaign is that the ad campaign goes away the minute you stop paying for it. A content marketing campaign lasts forever.

Knowing What Content Customers Want

Besides creating content about your products, what else can you create content about that your customers will find valuable? How do you know what your customers want?

The answers to these questions lie in the *Buyer Persona Worksheets* you completed in Chapter Two. The worksheets show you precisely what your audiences are looking for.

A quick refresher of our example from Chapter Two: In completing the *Buyer Persona Worksheet* for the small electrical contractor, we came up with the following five goals:

- Build a successful small business that provides for his family
- Provide value to his customers and build a strong relationship with them
- Manage his time and his workers time efficiently and productively
- Eventually sell the business
- Stay up to date with the building code and new technologies

We also came up with the following five challenges:

- Finding high-caliber employees who stick around
- Keeping up with technology
- Finding new customers/building his business
- Balancing inventory and cost
- Time management

The ten items above are also ten topics our electrical distributor can create content around, none of which includes product promotion. In fact, the topics listed above discuss issues that any (or every) small electrical contractor will likely be interested in learning about and so will search on at some point.

Writing about topics that are helpful to the contractor's business will attract the contractor to our distributor's site because this is information he would find valuable and want to learn more about.

It is safe to say, therefore, that any electrical distributor who writes about these or similar topics as opposed to writing about their products will be far ahead of the competition when it comes to being found online.

What Wouldn't be the Right Content to Publish?

There are certain topics you should avoid or downplay in a blog post or article. Rarely should your content brag about how wonderful your company is. Instead, carefully weave your company and your products into the content you develop but keep the flow of information geared toward the customer benefits.

For example, in a blog post about a solution your business offers, talk about how the solution helps customers and how it will save them time, money, headaches, etc. Give readers information that applies directly to *them*. Avoid including self-serving details and platitudes.

Before sharing information, always remember to ask yourself, "What's in it for the customer?" For every piece of content you produce, be sure to make the benefits abundantly clear. Customers don't always recognize why products and services are valuable to them. Readers will often miss the connection between an offering and themselves.

In producing content, what is evident to you, the content producer, isn't always apparent to readers, so it is better to overstate the benefits than to understate them. As mentioned in Chapter Two, use clear statements such as: "We are here to help you by offering you X, and this is why X is of value to you"; *or* "By offering you X, we are helping you in a way our competitors cannot. Here is how it will help you."

Staying Connected to Customers in Your Sales Funnel

Above, we covered two very different ways to create content. We talked about creating content that provides educational information that will help get your business noticed (e.g., simple product videos). We also talked about creating content that laser-targets your audiences' goals and challenges (e.g., writing about the topics revealed in your *Buyer Persona Worksheets*). Which should you create and why? The easy answer is that you should create *all* of it. The more you create, the better.

But there is more to content marketing that simply creating and publishing content. In fact, there is a proven and methodical way to present your content so that it moves people forward more quickly through your sales funnel. We will explore how this is done throughout the rest of this chapter.

To begin with, timing is significant when it comes to content marketing. The content prospects see during their buyer's journey should correlate to where they are in the sales funnel. Targeting content to the appropriate stage in the buyer's journey can be difficult, and each buyer's journey is different. Most companies write content, post it, and *hope* that the right person sees it at the right time.

Instead of merely hoping, present your content so that specific pieces appear at predetermined points in time during a buyer's journey. Arranging your content this way will help ensure that when prospects see a piece of content that strikes a chord with them, they are moved closer to a sale.

Timing content and correlating the content's message, more commonly referred to as *content mapping*, helps control each prospect's attention as he moves through the buyer's journey. It is the process of planning or mapping a buyer's journey and creating and sharing pieces of content—like leaving a trail of breadcrumbs—that brings your buyers through the sales funnel and closer to a purchase. You will work through content mapping shortly using the *Content Mapping Worksheet*, but first, let's go over the various stages in a buyer's journey.

Attract and Educate Buyers in the Awareness Stage

Depending on who you ask, a typical buyer's journey can have anywhere from three to eight stages. I tend to focus on four and will do so in this book.

The first stage is awareness. The awareness stage is the point in time when your prospective buyers realize and have expressed symptoms of a potential problem (or opportunity). These buyers don't know they have a problem, or they don't know what the problem is, only that something isn't right; the buyers in the awareness stage have some *uncomfortableness*. They are feeling certain symptoms. They will search the internet to resolve their situation, but those searches will center on the *symptoms* their companies are experiencing. They will not be searching for exact solutions (yet) because they do not yet know what they need.

The most effective way to connect with buyers in the awareness stage is with content about their symptoms, which will strategically guide them (again, think breadcrumbs) from their symptoms to their solution. The awareness stage is not the time to spring a solution on a buyer. It's too early in their journey. If buyers come across information about solutions that do not directly tie to their symptoms, your messaging may not resonate with them. They may not recognize the solution as *their* solution because these buyers won't yet realize what their actual problems are.

The awareness stage is where you'll begin to draw an imaginary line connecting the buyers' symptoms to various problems and solutions. Using the content presented at the awareness stage, you will gather telling information about your buyer, and you will also guide buyers closer to your solutions.

Say you are a plumbing supplies distributor who offers vendor-managed inventory solutions, and you would like to find more customers for that solution, including Joe Smith, who already buys some of his plumbing supplies from you. Here is an example of how Joe's buyer's journey may go:

Joe Smith is a commercial plumber who has four or five trucks and between ten and fifteen employees. Most of his employees are on the road, and he has a few part-timers who help maintain the shop, keep the trucks stocked up, and order products when needed. He believes he is paying too much in labor, so he has embarked on a mission to figure out how to reduce labor costs.

Does Joe need a vendor-managed inventory solution? Maybe. But if you ask him right now, he will tell you no. Right now, he thinks his workers are just wasting time.

One day Joe reads an article on your website called, "Time is Money: Six Tips to Creating a More Efficient Plumbing Business." The article talks about various systems that help plumbers run their businesses more efficiently. One of the tips in the article is about reducing paperwork. Another tip is about using new technology. There is also a tip about organizing inventory with a VMI solution.

As a result of the article, Joe does a bit more research on new technologies. He likes what he reads and purchases a GPS for each truck. Because a big piece of his business is emergency service, he believes he spends too much time tracking down and dispatching his fleet to service calls. He implements the tracking system, which allows him to see where everyone is at all times; and as a result, he has reduced the number of dispatch calls to his drivers from an average of fifty or sixty per day to fewer than fifteen per day.

Immediately he feels as though his business is running more efficiently and that he has saved time and money. That is until he processes the next payroll. He sees that although the GPS saves time with dispatching, his workers still were clocking longer-than-expected hours. Nevertheless, Joe believes the tracking system was a worthwhile investment. It allows him to keep an eye on how his workers spend their time. He can print out a stop report for each driver at the end of each week, showing every arrival and departure time, which puts him a step closer to figuring out why his workers are racking up hours.

In reviewing the stop reports, Joe notices that two of his workers take longer than usual lunches several times a week. It makes him a bit angry, but it's an easy fix. But what Joe also discovers makes him even angrier: Joe sees that his drivers spend a lot of time at his distributor's will-call counter. In fact, they visit the counter at least four or five times each week, and some visit the counter more than once a day. And, he notices, some of these stops take up to 45 minutes or longer. Joe looks around his office at the stacks of receipts and thinks about how he had asked his guys to place their parts orders themselves and pick up their supplies on their way to their jobs.

He suddenly realizes he has a bigger problem than he thought. Not only does he discover why he spends so much in labor, but also, more troublesome, he realizes his guys are purchasing supplies that are not being tracked. He wonders if his guys are stealing from him.

That night, he brings home the stacks of receipts, and he and his wife spend the night entering them into a spreadsheet and cross-matching them to jobs. Happily, they match every receipt to a job, but he realizes things could have turned out much differently. He knows he must do something to keep better control of his inventory.

Note how Joe is zeroing in on his problem (inflated labor costs + inventory issues). He started out in the awareness stage of the buyer's journey, looking for ways to save payroll costs. As he draws closer to the real problem, he enters the consideration stage.

Attract and Educate Buyers in the Consideration Stage

In the consideration stage, prospects are closer to understanding their specific problem. But since most problems have more than one solution, this is the stage where buyers would consider their options. Let's go back to Joe:

Joe initially thought he had a payroll / time-management issue. In addressing that issue, he discovered he had a more serious problem—inventory management. His original symptoms were higher-than-expected labor costs and time wasted on dispatch calls. He's happy he has been able to reduce time spent on dispatching, but he realizes his real problem with labor costs ties into his shop's inventory situation.

Again, he starts researching. He does some searching on the internet, reads some articles, talks to a few of his plumbing buddies on social media, and eventually sits down with his wife during dinner to weigh their options.

"Maybe we should look at changing suppliers. Some distributors have paperless order systems that let us match orders directly to our jobs using the computer. A solution like that may make inventory easier to track."

"Or perhaps we should stock a larger physical inventory in house. This way we can reduce the number of trips to the will-call counter. But do we have the resources to manage so much inventory?"

"Maybe we can find a software program we can plug into to help us manage our inventory. I'll ask my current supplier if he knows what other plumbers do to handle this issue."

In a perfect world, because Joe already buys plumbing supplies from your distributorship, he might call you the next day, and you would tell him about the various VMI programs your company offers. But it's Friday night, and Joe turns to the internet instead.

Joe searches for "best ways for plumbers to manage inventory," and finds an article entitled, "3 Inventory Management Tips for Plumbing and HVAC Contractors."

The article Joe found is the perfect article for a candidate for a VMI program, especially one who is at the consideration stage in their buyer's journey. But, while it's a win for Joe that he found the article, it's a loss for you because that article is sitting on your competitor's website. Back to Joe:

Because Joe is your customer, he decides to visit your website directly to see if there is any information there about inventory management. He doesn't recall ever seeing any, but he does recall your article "Time is Money: Six Tips to Creating a More Efficient Plumbing Business," and he remembers that VMI was mentioned in it.

When he pulls up the article a second time, he notices that the tip about VMI links to a handful of case studies your company published about customer successes with your inventory management solutions. Joe is happy to learn that you do, in fact, offer VMI programs and sends you an email asking you to call him on Monday morning.

When prospects are in the consideration stage, they are considering their options. This is the stage in the buying process when your salesperson would talk about the pros and cons of all the solutions your business offers. He'd talk about the various benefits each solution offers, and he might offer advice about some of the other options a prospect is considering. He may even make a comparison showing the benefits of your various managed inventory solutions versus some of their other choices.

But when a salesperson cannot get in front of the prospect or the prospect conducts research on his own, your content must fill that gap, which is exactly what your case studies did in this example.

Convert the Sale in the Acquisition Stage

Buyers who are close to a purchase are found toward the bottom of a typical sales funnel. It is at this point in the buyer's journey where your sales team plays its most relevant role. During the acquisition stage, buyers have decided on the product(s) or solution(s) that best suit their needs, and they are ready to "pull the trigger" and make a purchase.

Since in the acquisition stage buyers have a strong idea about the solutions they are looking for, they will look more closely at attributes such as brand, size, price, features, and, of course, where they will purchase the items or services they've decided on. They will likely base their purchases on price *if there are no other variables to consider*, so the content found at the acquisition stage should be more detailed and highlight the benefits of specific products, services, or solutions (vs. being about a pain-point or a struggle of the buyer). *Content found at this stage should make the argument about why a product or service should be purchased from you.*

Piggybacking off the example above, Joe is now at the bottom of the sales funnel, ready to buy. He knows he wants an inventory management program; it's the solution he's decided to put in place. It's time for your salesperson to convince Joe that he should purchase a program from you, so here is where your salesperson would share with Joe the marketing collateral that emphasizes the various attributes and advantages of each of the VMI programs your company offers as well as any information about your company itself that may move him toward a purchase.

If your salesperson could get in front of Joe, he would know exactly what to say and share to close the deal. But in case Joe decides to do more research before speaking with your salesperson, you must be sure information is available to him that helps him learn more about your VMI programs and your company.

At this stage, therefore, you'll *(finally!)* present marketing collateral that *is* all about your business. Collateral found at the acquisition stage should do a brilliant job of demonstrating why your VMI programs are the best and how your company will help Joe pick the right VMI program for his business. You may also include information at the acquisition stage that discusses cost savings, your company's attention to detail, and the high level of customer service you deliver to your happy customers.

The acquisition stage is the time to sell based on why *your* company is the one to choose for a managed inventory system; you don't have to sell them on the fundamental idea of a managed inventory program itself anymore. Now is the time to convince your prospects that working with your company is their smartest choice.

Upsell and Strengthen Your Relationship in the Loyalty Stage

Most distributors direct very little sales and marketing toward their customers after the acquisition stage. It's unfortunate because the loyalty stage is where you have the best opportunity to gain a larger share of customer spend. For companies who wish to align themselves with their customers' success (like you if you're reading this book), you must think of your sales cycle as less of a funnel and more as a flywheel.

> *The traditional metaphor for sales is the "funnel." But today, a better metaphor is the "flywheel." The actual flywheel was used by James Watt over 200 years ago in his steam engine, the invention that powered the Industrial Revolution. It is highly efficient at capturing, storing, and releasing energy.*
>
> *Using a flywheel to describe sales allows leaders to focus on how we capture, store, and release energy, as measured in traffic and leads, freemium sign-ups, new customers, and the enthusiasm of existing customers. It's got a sense of leverage and momentum. The metaphor also accounts for loss of energy, where lost users and customers work against momentum and slow growth.[6]*

The loyalty stage is also known as the service stage. The loyalty stage gives you an opportunity to dazzle customers, and when done well, they send you referrals. That's the energy Schwartzman is referring to above. It is also during this stage that you would collect testimonials and start to build case studies. One of the most fruitful strategies that occurs at this stage, and would keep the forward momentum going, would be to simply follow up with customers periodically to ensure their continued satisfaction and enquire about how else you could serve them.

To keep customers loyal, a distributor may offer some form of discount, put customers in a loyalty program, check in with customers regularly, and identify other issues a customer may have that the distributor can help with. During the loyalty stage, your goal should be to strengthen your relationship with your customers.

---

6   Schwartzman, Eric. "2021 Guide to B2B Content Marketing." *EricSchwartzman.com*. https://www. ericschwartzman.com/why-b2b-content-marketing-is-important. Accessed April 2021.

How about your business? Do you have loyalty programs in place that strengthen your customer relationships and build trust? Complete the *Loyalty Stage Audit Sheet* to examine the programs you have in place. Discuss the effectiveness of each program and ensure there is a program for each target audience you would like to attract and retain. Capture and discuss new ideas as well.

Side note: Since Joe was already your customer, he was technically in the loyalty stage, but there didn't seem to be much of a relationship there beyond his occasional purchases. Had a salesperson been closer to Joe, his need for a VMI program might have revealed itself much sooner!

The Importance of Content Mapping

Now that we've clarified the stages of a typical sales cycle and how to address each of them, you can see the differences in the information to promote at each stage and why.

The concept of mapping content to the buyer's journey is relatively new in the distribution space. Distributors more commonly market directly to the acquisition stage and leave the other three stages to chance. But by ignoring stages one, two, and four, your company is missing a large swath of business and leaving money on the table to be grabbed up by the competition.

As demonstrated in Joe's story, you will attract more candidates for the products and solutions your business offers when you focus on a customers' symptoms first. The process to do so is simple: First, target prospects who are in the awareness stage with sales and marketing collateral focused on pain-points or struggles (i.e., symptoms of a larger problem). Doing so will draw those prospects in. Then, capture each prospect as a lead and nurture those leads through the consideration stage and into the acquisition stage. We'll talk about how to do this in Chapter Five. If all goes well, you will eventually land them as customers, at which point they will enter the loyalty/service stage where you can increase wallet-share from each by keeping in closer touch with them.

In addition to planning how and when to deploy various content pieces to match your buyer's journey, the content-mapping process will also identify any deficits in your content library. For example, as you plan out your content, you may discover you don't have any case studies. In that event, the marketing and sales teams would work together to create some.

Look at the *Content Mapping Worksheets* in your supplemental materials. Note that there are three versions — A version with instructions, a sample version that's already been filled out for you, and a blank version for you to complete. Start slowly, concentrating on just one buyer persona at a time, and work your way through the sheet. The content-mapping process is tricky, so be patient and do your best. All the worksheets can be updated as you move forward and begin to get a stronger understanding of how to map out your content and what each piece of content should achieve.

Outbound Marketing and How it can Help You

We talked a lot about inbound marketing here in Chapter Three. Inbound marketing, you will recall, is content marketing that focuses on a prospect's pain points, goals, and struggles and attracts prospects who are looking for solutions. Now let's talk about outbound marketing, which, if I were going to assign it a stage in the buyer's journey, I'd call it the *pre*-awareness stage.

Sales and marketing strategies that are considered to be outbound marketing would include:

- Events
- Trade shows
- Speaking engagements
- Direct mail
- Advertisements
- Magazine articles
- Cold calling

Using outbound sales and marketing strategies or tactics allows you to target prospects who might never have heard of you otherwise. Chances are these prospects weren't looking for your company or your products or even any solutions, but they have somehow come across you, and you've gotten their attention.

Outbound marketing is like fishing. You cast a line, whether it is by having a table at a trade show or mailing a postcard, and you hope to hook someone's attention and reel them in.

Because the prospects you attract via outbound marketing were not deliberately seeking you or seeking a solution, you must give them a reason to either purchase right away, or you must ensure they will remember your company when they are ready to make a purchase. The best way to stay top-of-mind is to put a strong follow-up campaign in place that includes a proven cadence of touch points including email, the occasional phone call, and consistently providing them with valuable information. We'll address follow-up in Chapter Five.

CHAPTER 4

Choosing the Right Technology

"AI and machine learning will give you the ability to automate manual processes that involve data and decision-making, giving you the ability to understand and act on data-driven insights with greater speed and efficiency." [7]

Artificial intelligence and machine learning - stealthy yet intriguing terms that promise to deliver massive success. These terms are everywhere. Every software company, including those that have been around for decades, is now hanging its hat on their AI and machine learning capabilities. It's almost impossible to remember what some of these companies delivered to us before AI and machine learning arrived on the scene.

Artificial intelligence (AI) and machine learning have been making our personal lives easier for years now. This is not something new

---

7   https://ai.engineering.columbia.edu/ai-vs-machine-learning/

and there's nothing remarkable about it. Not anymore. From Google pre-populating our search bars, to Netflix recommending movies to us, to getting the latest weather report from Alexa, technology has perfected the personalization of our everyday world. This is machine learning in its simplest form.

When artificial intelligence and machine learning first hit the scene, it was a difficult option for distributors to take part in because the cost was extremely prohibitive. Eventually, like every other technological advancement, with time costs to implement AI and machine learning have become much more affordable and cost effective.

In fact, AI and machine learning have become so commonplace, that today we're seeing more and more data-driven, distribution-specific solutions appear. These data-driven solutions are allowing distributors to adopt AI and machine learning at just a fraction of the cost and effort compared to just three or four years ago.

So just exactly what is artificial intelligence, and how is it different from machine learning?

According to The Fu Foundation School of Engineering and Applied Science at Columbia University, artificial intelligence and machine learning are often used interchangeably, but machine learning is actually a subset of AI. They write the following:

> *"Put in context, artificial intelligence (AI) refers to the general ability of computers to emulate human thought and perform tasks in real-world environments, while machine learning refers to the technologies and algorithms that enable systems to identify patterns, make decisions, and improve themselves through experience and data.*
>
> *Artificial Intelligence is the field of developing computers and robots that are capable of behaving in ways that both mimic*

and go beyond human capabilities. AI-enabled programs can analyze and contextualize data to provide information or automatically trigger actions without human interference.

Machine learning is a pathway to artificial intelligence. This subcategory of AI uses algorithms to automatically learn insights and recognize patterns from data, applying that learning to make increasingly better decisions.

Deep learning, an advanced method of machine learning, goes a step further. Deep learning models use large neural networks — networks that function like a human brain to logically analyze data — to learn complex patterns and make predictions independent of human input."[8]

How Distributors Can Best Leverage Technology

In planning out your digital future, and to support your long-range business objectives, it would be foolish for any company *not* to explore multiple solutions and technologies. It's important to have a clear understanding of what you will need both now and for the long-term viability of your business. Because technology presents a multitude of options that evolve very quickly, the more knowledgeable you are about what's available to you, the better positioned you will be to make decisions in the future.

The key to success when it comes to anything data-related is tied directly to your company's ability to transform your data into actionable insights you can use to run your business at its maximum potential.

This could include using digital strategies to automate tasks and processes, using marketing automation to track the behavior of your buyers and their interest in your products, using machine learning to increase productivity, and using artificial intelligence to forewarn

---

8   https://ai.engineering.columbia.edu/ai-vs-machine-learning/

you of a danger or predict success with a certain direction you'd like to move in.

Faster Access to Better Information

Infor's Coleman, built off their core technology and cloud services, is an artificial intelligence platform that has both proactive and predictive capabilities. It has digital assistance capabilities utilizing natural language processing (NLP) so you can engage it with text or voice. It stays always available as a persistent user (think Siri and Alexa), and it stands ready to assist with any tasks or respond to questions that can be answered through an analysis of your data.

Coleman's output ranges in levels of sophistication, from responding to simple queries to something much more complicated, such as predicting events and proactively alerting users to activities that require attention. An example of the latter would be executing predictive maintenance on products, ensuring the necessary equipment is on hand to make repairs before a problem even occurs.

Identifying New Opportunities for Growth

The more sales channels you deploy, the more data there is to manage (think eCommerce, sales counters, emails to a CSR, visits from an OSR, marketplaces, etc.). Factor in the hundreds, maybe thousands of customers your distributorship handles, along with the number of products you sell, and it's no wonder that distributors have a hard time proactively cross-selling and upselling. Even a tenured sales rep will struggle to find the information to help build a deeper, more consultative relationship with the customer.

When a sales rep believes it's time to solicit a re-order, which may or may not be the right time by the way, often he'll have no real insight around what the customer needs or may want beyond their initial, routine order. The sales rep will offer the same products the customer has been purchasing for years and often nothing more.

We're seeing artificial intelligence unblocking these challenges at scale using products like Proton, a software developed for distributors that has combined AI modeling and natural language processing. Proton was developed to give distributors easy access in real time to insights such as which items a customer needs at what time, or when it's time to reorder products.

The unified data Proton makes available helps distributors predict who is going to buy what as well as when they're going to buy. This, in turn, gives distributors the ability to prepare a more coordinated sales strategy across channels. Sales reps can have better-informed conversations with their customers and make product recommendations that are much more relevant to the customer – information that reveals the wallet share gaps that exist for each specific customer and gives the salesperson the insight to fill those gaps.

The benefits to a distributor using Proton are twofold. The first, of course, is that the sales team is more knowledgeable about the customers' needs and buying behaviors and can therefore be better prepared for sales calls.

The second benefit, which I believe is just as important, is that your customers will have a much better buying experience when dealing with a well-informed salesperson. Because of heightened competition in the distribution industry, a positive customer experience is more important today than it's ever been.

Recognize and Cultivate Your Most Valuable Leads

We've already discussed the need to break out of the silos often found in distribution in order to become more productive, and using technology is the most efficient way to do so. To meet the unique needs and requirements of the distribution and manufacturing industries, LeadSmart Technologies has developed LeadSmart Channel Cloud™, a vertical-specific, purpose-built CRM and Business Intelligence platform. LeadSmart's focus is on providing tools, insights, ERP integration and marketing automation capabilities that help drive sales growth while also providing value to sales teams, marketing teams, management, and executives.

While most CRMs are "one size fits all," LeadSmart Channel Cloud was built specifically for distribution related companies.

Something unique about LeadSmart is that it allows distribution companies to track activities with not just their buyers, but also with specific sales agents, key vendors, and other partners. Distributors using LeadSmart's unique capabilities have access to valuable insights into partner activity, relationship strength, and various ways to expand revenue based on the data LeadSmart generates.

Automate Sales-Related Tasks and Processes

Marketing automation is a catch-all phrase that refers to software platforms and technologies designed to effectively share digital sales and marketing collateral. Some of the basic marketing automation functions include email, social media posting, and list-building activities. The intention of these basic features is to streamline and simplify some of the most time-consuming and repetitive tasks involved with digital sales and marketing.

Marketing automation platforms will also track and collect data across multiple online channels, allowing you to quickly capture and identify leads, and then measure the viability of these leads based on demographics and buyer behavior. Marketing automation also allows you to quickly recognize which digital strategies are most effective at moving your prospects closer to a purchase.

> *"Customer journeys are the sum of individual personalized experiences with your brand. With marketing automation, you can tailor every interaction based on customer data to create ongoing, seamless journeys through every brand touchpoint. Marketing automation creates relevant content and messaging at scale across many channels. Generate digital ads that appear for the right person at the right time. Recommend the right products on your website for each individual user — automatically.*
>
> *With marketing automation, you can reach customers along their journey no matter where they are in the customer lifecycle — from acquisition to advocacy. Deliver timely, relevant content that reaches customers when, where, and how they prefer — converting prospects into lifelong brand advocates."[9]*

In previous chapters, we talked about using digital sales and marketing collateral to deliberately moves your buyers closer to a sale. We also talked about using tracking software and/or a CRM to keeps tabs on where each buyer is in the sales cycle, giving you a greater ability to capture and hold the attention of your buyers and move them closer to a purchase. Your marketing automation system is what you'll use to do exactly that.

Marketing automation systems come in many sizes, and each has its own sets of features and benefits. As mentioned earlier, robust marketing automation systems will support your sales function by identifying audiences, deploying content, and triggering actions or notifications for your salespeople based on buyer behavior.

---

9   Sweezey, Matthew. "What is Marketing Automation?" *Salesforce.com.* https://www.salesforce.com/products/marketing-cloud/what-is-marketing-automation/ Accessed April 2021.

Marketing automation can capture, nurture, track and score your leads, and then integrate those leads seamlessly into your CRM, giving your salespeople the 'intel' it needs to close a sale. Marketing and sales departments use marketing automation in conjunction with their CRM to automate online marketing campaigns and sales activities to both increase revenue and maximize efficiency.

Which Marketing Automation System is Best for You?

Every company should be using marketing automation. To get started, choose a system appropriate in size and function to meet your immediate needs as well as what you foresee your company needing in the next twelve to eighteen months. From there, as your digital sales and marketing endeavors grow, it will become obvious when it's time for you to explore a more robust platform.

Some of the more exciting marketing automation features to consider that also add value to a CRM system include:

- Capturing leads and helping with follow-up
- Promoting and sharing sales and marketing collateral based on prospect behavior and interests
- Identifying anonymous website traffic
- Connecting with prospects via social media
- Qualifying and prioritizing leads in the sales pipeline
- Segmenting lists of prospects and customers based on their behaviors and attributes
- Analyzing granular data that will measure levels of successful campaigns and guide the sales and marketing teams' focus
- Tracking visitor behavior on your website, learning about who visited (name, company name, email address, and more),

what they looked at, which pages they visited, and how long they lingered

- Alerting your salespeople with helpful information that indicates a buyer is moving closer to a purchase

How Marketing Automation Supports Your Sales Function

Your marketing automation systems can be a reliable collector of customer data, and some marketing automation systems collect more information than others. Data collected and aggregated can include information about a visitor's activities on your website, but also, depending on the system you're using, can provide you with visitor activities on other sites as well. The information collected includes the pages they view, the ads they click, the operating systems visitors use, when they visited, what actions they took, their IP address and more.

Collecting data is particularly important because your data will help segment your audience and direct the buying journeys that lead to your products and services.

Let's talk a bit about why segmenting your audience using marketing automation is effective. When a link about a particular subject is clicked, whether in an email or on your website, your automation system can add those who clicked the link to an audience segment (basically a list) to whom, from there, you might deploy more information about that topic.

Returning visitors will often find their name and email address already pre-populated in forms that encourage them to download or access additional media. This is a perfect opportunity to ask for another piece of data, such as their title or company name. Moving forward, through even more visits, additional demographic data can be asked for such as revenue, headcount, location, and any other data that would allow you to better classify them. How does this speed up the sales cycle?

You might ask for someone's title, from which you can determine their decision-making authority. You might ask for the number of employees they have and their revenue to determine whether they are a candidate for a product or service your business offers. This practice is known as progressive profiling, and it is a very effective method of lead prequalification.

As mentioned above, marketing automation also gives you the ability to measure the success of your digital sales and marketing efforts. Knowing that a substantial number of your email recipients clicked a particular link indicates that the information shared is interesting or valuable. With marketing automation (and in a sense, anything that is digital, really), you will be able to measure KPIs that show which strategies perform well and which do not. Having the ability to measure your results, in turn, will help you decide which campaigns you should do more of and which you should probably do less of. We'll talk more about this in Chapter Six.

What's New in Marketing Automation and Why it Matters

The sharing of your data across your individual tech platforms will be critical to not only your sales success, but also to your ability to serve your customers. Therefore, as you start your journey in choosing your marketing automation system, it is important that you understand how powerful and relevant to a company's sales and marketing efforts data and data management systems have become.

Some of the largest software companies and CRM systems have teamed up with marketing automation and AI software companies to form vast repositories of personal and professional data. These companies sell access to that data via subscription which, when used properly, can deliver substantial benefits to a customer that wants to boost their online sales strategy.

Digital Sales & Marketing Data

It would be helpful and probably important that you understand what's available to you vis-à-vis digital sales and marketing data along with its history. Here's a short overview.

In 2013, Salesforce, considered the world's number one CRM, purchased ExactTarget and Pardot, two marketing automation powerhouses. Since then, to build out their AI capabilities, Salesforce quickly acquired more than a dozen leading software companies in the data management and artificial intelligence arenas. *(Lucy Mazalon. "Top Salesforce Acquisitions of All-Time—Where Are They Now?")*

In 2019, they purchased Tableau Software, a big data firm that allows users to query and store multiple data sources and generate graph-like visualizations to help users interpret the data. In 2021, they purchased Slack Technologies, which is a leading project management and messaging software that facilitates easier project management and open, immediate communication internally between employees as well as internally and externally between a company and their customers.

In 2012, Oracle acquired Eloqua, a powerful marketing automation system. Then, in 2015, Oracle acquired Bronto, a marketing automation system commonly used for B2C e-commerce. Oracle then acquired NetSuite in 2016. Since then, and as of this writing, Oracle has acquired twenty or more additional software companies in their efforts to best serve its customers.

In 2018, Adobe, who is considered one of the world's largest and most diversified software companies, purchased Magento, a popular B2B eCommerce platform, and Marketo, a marketing automation dynamo and a fierce competitor of Salesforce's Pardot. Since then, they've also acquired software around 3D and gaming, a popular video collaboration software, and a well-known project management software with more than 3,000 customers and one million users. For years, Adobe has been a leader in digital design and creativity products, and today they are making unprecedented strides in the B2B data world.

The mergers and acquisitions mentioned above are significant because all three conglomerates possess an unfathomable amount of data, and all three conglomerates aim to use this data to give their customers the best 360-degree view into the leads in their databases, *in real time.*

So, what exactly does that mean? Let's use Salesforce to illustrate this concept.

Salesforce began as a simple customer relationship management (CRM) program in 1999. As of this writing, they are a global leader with over 56,000 employees and 150,000 customers. Eighty-three percent of Fortune 500 companies use Salesforce. They have evolved over the years into what is probably the world's most robust sales, marketing, and business development platform.

Not very long ago, Salesforce allowed non-Salesforce customers to 'buy' customer data from them by trading it for data that Salesforce didn't yet have. For example, if I had your contact information (i.e., name, email address, phone number, title, and company name) in my possession, and if you were not already in Salesforce's database, I could trade your information with Salesforce in return for someone's contact information I wanted but did not yet have.

Salesforce's practice of trading contact information ended in May 2019, but by then it had already significantly expanded the amount of data in their possession. On top of that, each of their acquisitions mentioned above brought their own sets of data to expand Salesforce's database even further. Now, instead of trading data, Salesforce users and users of their subsidiaries can subscribe to it.

If I use Pardot as my marketing automation system, and a stranger—someone who has never visited before and with whom I've never interacted—visits my website, I can identify that visitor if his contact information is already in any of Salesforce's companies' databases *if I subscribe to that data sharing service.* Pardot will capture the visitor's IP address and then cross-reference that IP address with the databases under Salesforce's umbrella and will add the visitor's name, title, company name, phone number, email address, and almost any other public-facing information available about that visitor into *my* Pardot account.

Based on my subscriptions to Salesforce data and other data providers, it quite possibly would also allow me to keep tabs on this visitor as he visits other websites as well.

Suppose I learn the following week that this visitor signed up for a webinar at a competitor's site. I would then know a bit more about what my visitor is interested in or shopping for, and better target them as a possible prospect for my services. Or, say he's got a contract with a competitor that will be expiring soon. I may be able to access that information as well and target him with services that I know are up for grabs.

In essence, these and other data conglomerates allow their customers to access information from their databases based on whatever plan their customers subscribe to. This data gives its subscribers a 360-degree view of any person or business that crosses the subscriber's path. That's powerful.

As a result, subscribers of these services get enriched profiles that automatically update in real time, allowing them to react instantly to customer events (behaviors) and immediately deliver relevant experiences via web, email, mobile, social, and more through the CDPs (customer data platforms) these data empires provide.

How Automation Can Help You Meet Your Sales Goals

Marketing automation is not a one-size-fits-all proposition. Every distributor has their own unique situation to consider when choosing marketing automation. A logical course of action would be to start slowly, monitor your use, and grow from there.

Assessing where you are now and where you would like to be eighteen months from now is a good way to start. Choose a platform or suite of tools to get your feet wet as you learn the concepts and identify which features your business will use most often.

When choosing your marketing automation platform and the software features you would like to have, here are some features and benefits to consider:

- Would you like to capture, follow up, and nurture leads using segmenting information specifically based on their interests? Or are you okay with your leads being bucketed onto one list and receiving identical communicates regardless of segments?

- Would you like to identify anonymous website traffic? More than 90% of your website visitors leave without making a purchase. Would you like to know who they are?

- Would you like to connect with prospects via social media? Getting traction via social media is a challenging venue for distributors, but some tactics work!

- Is qualifying and prioritizing the leads in your sales pipeline important to your sales process right now?

- Is personalization important to your sales and marketing strategy? Would the ability to segment your audiences based on their behaviors and their attributes be of value to you?

- Do you wonder where your marketing dollars are going? Analyzing the granular data provided by marketing automation will help you measure and guide the sales and marketing teams' focus.

- Is the ability to distribute sales and marketing collateral based on a prospect's behavior and interests an ability you would like to have? Do you believe it is vital that you get the right information to the right person at the right time in the format that is most appealing to them?

- When prospects visit your website, would you like to know that they visited, what they looked at, which pages they spent time on, and how long they stayed on each page? Would that knowledge give your salespeople more insight into each prospect and what the prospect is looking for?

Here is an example of a notification that Marketo, Adobe's marketing automation system, would send to a salesperson when a lead visits his website:

FOR INTERNAL USE ONLY

Joe Smith from **Acme Electric** has been actively engaging with **Electrical Safety** digital marketing campaign launched **3/21/22** and is now a **HOT CONTACT**.

They became a Hot Contact with a **Lead Score of 105** by completing this/these activities:
- Clicked on a link in the **3/21/22 email w/subject line: How to Mitigate Risk on the Job**
- Spent **13** minutes on **page w/title: industrial-safety-solutions**
- Clicked on link to **page w/title: safety-motor-control**
- Filled out form to download **eBook w/title: Protect Personnel from an Arc Flash Event**
- Clicked on link in email to access **eBook w/title: Protect Personnel from an Arc Flash Event**

<u>Your Action Items:</u>

1. Review **Joe Smith**'s record in MSI to see what other <u>websites</u>, <u>emails</u>, <u>virtual events</u>, and <u>webinars</u> they have been engaging with. Look for important insights that can help inform your next conversation.

2. <u>Accept</u> or <u>disqualify</u> this MQL by responding back to this email. Please <u>accept</u> if this is a viable opportunity.

3. Follow up! Per company standard, **please follow up with Joe Smith within 72 hours.**

<u>Hot Contact Details:</u>
Name: Joe Smith
Business Name: Acme Electric
Email Address: joe.smith@acmeelectric.net
Telephone: 543-210-9876
<u>Link to CRM/MSI record</u>
<u>Link to Account</u>

Last activity date: **3/29/22**

Would a notification like this one be effective in your organization?

Here's an example of how I've used these notifications here in my business:

One morning, I sent an email to a list of distributors. The email contained a link back to my website, where I had just published an article. I programmed my marketing automation system to notify me when someone clicked the link to read the article.

One notification in particular caught my attention. It told me the CEO of a large distribution company I'd recently met and had started a conversation with had clicked the link. We'd already established a good rapport, so I immediately gave him a call.

Imagine his surprise when, while he was reading my article, I happened to call him!

So as not to freak him out, I quickly explained that I knew he was on my site because of my marketing automation system, which he found to be quite impressive. That phone call led to an appointment with his sales and marketing teams, which eventually led to a long-standing, very important customer relationship.

Why Collecting and Nurturing Leads Matters

As mentioned earlier, it's estimated that 90% of website visitors leave without taking action. Visitors jump from website to website, learning about companies, researching products and services, and comparing prices. Website visitors are self-directed. They can find any information they are looking for, certainly enough to make a purchasing decision, if they look hard enough.

So how can you possibly speed up the sales cycle and have them engage with you sooner in the buying process?

The smartest and most effective strategy would be to build out a content marketing strategy by adding valuable, helpful content (as discussed in Chapter Three) to your website with a method to capture visitors' contact information (i.e., leads). From there you would nurture these leads through their buyer's journey to convert them into warm leads using marketing automation, which we'll discuss in Chapter Five.

A content marketing strategy only gets more effective over time (remember the lap joint flanges video). Information that's helpful in solving the problems your personas are dealing with will be considered valuable for a long time to come. When you share content on a regular basis, you'll see it build into a powerful library of helpful information about solutions that people search for and will continue to search for. As your library of content grows, it will attract more and more visitors to your website.

Take Advantage of Some Key Benefits

Marketing automation systems are filled with 'must-haves' and 'nice to haves.' Let's talk about the must-haves. One of the most significant benefits of marketing automation, which is within reach of anyone who uses even the smallest systems, is the ability to target customers with personalized, valuable communications that are tailored to their interests. As you may recall from previous chapters, a worthwhile goal for your digital sales and marketing campaigns would be to know what interests your audience and provide them with that information.

Today, most distributors share information that they *think* their customers might be interested in. Sometimes the distributor hits the target, but more often, they do not. And when you miss the target, you run the risk of losing those customers or prospects; they may avoid opening future mail from your business or they may unsubscribe altogether. Sharing information that doesn't interest a customer or prospect sends a clear message that your company isn't in touch with the customer's wants, needs, struggles, or goals and it could hurt your relationship with them.

On the other hand, sharing information a reader feels is valuable and directed specifically to him implies that your company is customer-centric. It shows you have invested time and effort in learning who the customer is and what they need. Marketing automation makes personalization very easy to do. It facilitates the kind of personalization people have come to expect, making those one-to-one conversations with large customer bases possible.

Suppose your company has a large customer base of plumbing contractors. You might segment them according to shared goals or attributes — commercial plumbers vs. residential plumbers; or plumbers with employees, a storefront, and a fleet of trucks vs. the plumber who works from his home. In doing so, you can then create personalized, one-to-one digital conversations by communicating information that appeals to them specifically. Taking the time to personalize your communications will drive more sales so long as those communications are valuable to the recipient.

Another must-have is the ability to capture and then follow up with a lead. Look at the number of people who visit your website each month and compare it to the number of visitors who turned into leads. Is it a digestible ratio? If not, think about how much more valuable your website would be if you could turn more of those visitors into leads you could nurture automatically over time.

When deciding which marketing automation system would work for you, look at the sales and marketing campaigns you have launched over the past year. Do you know which campaigns have been the most successful? Do you know which campaigns have generated the most sales? A basic marketing automation system would help answer such questions which, in turn, would help guide you toward doing more of what worked and less of what didn't work.

While all the capabilities and scenarios mentioned in this chapter are attractive, be careful not to put the cart before the horse. Start with the must-haves and work toward outgrowing that system to the point where you need and can justify a system containing 'nice-to-haves.' It's not difficult to change marketing automation systems as you grow. Create a goal and a realistic timeline to put each strategy in place. Be mindful of any long-term contracts you might be talked into, and as you grow your efforts adjust your technology according to your goal.

There is an adage we've all heard (or said): "Fifty percent of our marketing works—we just don't know which 50%." Marketing automation makes that statement obsolete. Using the simplest marketing automation systems, you can quickly learn what was successful and then zero in on *why* it was successful. Having this knowledge allows you to do more of what works to keep your sales pipeline filled.

Five Easy Ways to Begin Using Marketing Automation

This chapter certainly contains a lot of information, and perhaps it may have added more questions than it answered. The truth is most marketing automation platforms have many bells and whistles the average distributor will never use. But you do have to get started nonetheless!

To help get you started, below is a list of easy-to-implement tools and features to consider when you are ready to dip your toe in the waters of marketing automation.

1. Analytics

Use marketing automation first and foremost for the analytics it gathers. One of the most valuable benefits of the digital world is the ability you are given to capture data. Data, of course, can be measured; and anything that can be measured can be improved.

The analytics that marketing automation provides are not just for individual pieces of content like email and blogs. They can also give you cumulative results, allowing you to monitor how your results are progressing over time. Analytics would also paint a clearer picture of your buyers by giving you an understanding that you wouldn't ordinarily have about buyer behaviors on your website. Knowing the top links that each of your visitors clicked will tell you what they have looked at, which also tells you what they find valuable — the perfect topic to discuss at a customer's next sales call!

2. Live Chat and Chatbots

Chatbots have become quite intelligent over the past couple of years, and like most technology, they've become more affordable and easier to use. And, even more compelling, we're seeing an increase in companies finding great success with *live* chat.

Can live chat and chatbots help distributors? Absolutely! Live chat is a service you add to your website that you can monitor yourself, have a live operator monitor for you, or combine the two. Chatbots have been around a while, answering questions and providing standard information, and now we're seeing a steep elevation of capabilities with live chat.

With live chat on your website, US-based operators who are trained on your products and services and skilled at capturing leads monitor and engage with your website visitors around the clock. The live operators can answer specific questions, point buyers toward various products, or, even more impressive, these operators can connect an interested buyer directly to one of your salespeople via iMessage, telephone call, or an app.

As stated earlier, 90% of your website visitors leave without taking any action. Live chat changes this statistic dramatically.

Not ready for live chat? Chatbots will boost engagement and interactivity on your website as well. A chatbot will welcome visitors, and if the visitor is someone whose contact information you've captured previously, the chatbot will even address the visitor by name. It's an effective way to catch someone's attention.

When your live chat or chatbots are set up well, they will work in conjunction with the rest of your sales and marketing efforts and collateral. Typically, when visitors come to a website, the live chat operator or chatbot welcomes and engages them, offering assistance. Live chat operators and chatbots can be active all day or after hours, depending on your needs.

While a live chat operator is tasked specifically with capturing a lead and identifying their needs, a chatbot will ask questions and offer information, moving visitors further into the sales funnel by gathering more information about each visitor's hot buttons.

Your marketing automation system will capture the entire 'conversation' and track each visitor's path. That information then gets added to your CRM, which will notify your salesperson about the interaction. It can be very powerful.

3. Email Marketing

Email marketing is the most basic form of marketing automation. It has been around for a long time, and if your company has a customer list, chances are your marketing team has done some email marketing.

Email marketing can be as basic as sending out a newsletter to everyone in your database or as sophisticated as it being an initial first step in a complex workflow that segments a database and moves leads from cold to hot before funneling them to a salesperson to convert. It all depends on what resources an organization would like to allocate toward enhancing their sales processes.

An email can convince a recipient to take action, or it can irritate customers to the point of unsubscribing, so it is important to be mindful of how it's being used. Every business should use email marketing for the simple reason that it works. It is still the most effective method of digital marketing.

Unfortunately, many companies present their email in a one-size-fits-all format, which is where most recipients' frustrations stem from. People don't like spending time on irrelevant communications. When you segment your database and create messaging that includes helpful information to each individual segment, your recipients will look forward to hearing from your company and will happily open every email you send.

4. The Abandoned Shopping Cart

Another example of marketing automation in action is an abandoned shopping cart campaign. I am sure everyone who has shopped online has experienced the types of communications triggered from an abandoned shopping cart campaign at some point or another. It goes something like this:

You visit an eCommerce site and load up your shopping cart, get distracted, and click away from the site. A few hours later, you get an email reminding you that you have items in your cart. Some eCommerce sites will even send a coupon discounting those items to entice you to complete the purchase. If you have an eCommerce site, you are likely using an abandoned shopping cart campaign. If you are considering eCommerce or don't have an abandoned shopping cart campaign in your existing program, it would be a very effective strategy to add.

5. Lead Capture and Follow-up

Last but by no means least is marketing automation's ability to capture and follow up with leads. As mentioned earlier in this chapter, your ability to capture leads is probably the most important feature of marketing automation. To do so and then follow up with them automatically using personalized messaging is incredibly easy and efficient. Just think for a moment how difficult it would be to do so manually! Just about every marketing automation program under the sun will give your sales and marketing teams the ability to build simple lead capture capabilities.

I'll not go into the details about lead capture and follow-up here because it is so important to your strategy that I've devoted an entire chapter (Chapter Five) to it.

Choosing Your Marketing Automation System

Marketing automation can be a costly investment. Your organization obviously must consider the cost of the software, but you also should consider the manhours devoted to learning a new software system and loading in the data. It is important that, when choosing your system, you look at as much information as possible to make an educated decision.

In the Supplemental Materials (MDM.com/TDDBook), you will find several tools and guides to help you make an informed decision. The first is the *Marketing Automation Features Checklist*, which is a comprehensive list of the most commonly used features of marketing automation. Work through the list with your team and be sure to get everyone's input.

Once you have decided which features your company needs or would like to have, learn more about the various platforms that offer the features you are looking for by using the guidebooks in the Supplemental Materials. The first guidebook is titled *The Definitive Guide to Marketing Automation,* and it is published by Adobe. This guide will give you a seriously deep dive into the world of marketing automation, from the basics to the most complicated of workflows. You'll learn all you need to know from this guide including the many features and capabilities available today. As you might recall, Marketo is the marketing automation system provided by Adobe.

I've also included the *2022 Sales & Marketing Automation Comparison Guide* in the supplemental materials. This guide is published by SharpSpring, a powerful marketing automation provider that has recently been purchased by Constant Contact. The comparison guide compares six of the leading marketing automation vendors. It contains insightful and useful information about features and costs.

Visit MDM.com/TDDBook to download the Worksheets, Checklists, Agendas, Guidebooks, etc. referred to in this book.

CHAPTER 5

Managing Digital Leads

"As companies adopt digital sales and marketing strategies as a way to generate more leads, the importance of having an effective lead nurturing strategy becomes very clear. In most cases only a relatively small percentage of your inbound leads will be ready to make an immediate purchase, leaving upwards of 90% of your inbound leads on the table.

Implementing an effective lead nurturing strategy can have a huge impact on the results of your inbound marketing strategy, customer loyalty, customer retention, revenue, and more.

The process of nurturing leads involves purposefully engaging your target audience by offering relevant information, supporting them in any way they need, and maintaining a sense of delight throughout every stage of the buyer's journey.

Nurturing leads is critical to your business's success because these tactics directly impact a customer's decision about whether or not they want to convert into paying customers. There are a number of ways to nurture leads including targeted content, multi-channel nurturing, multiple touches, timely follow-ups, and personalization."[10]

10 Mawhinney, Jesse. "7 Amazingly Effective Lead Nurturing Tactics". *Hubspot.com*. Updated March 2020. https://blog.hubspot.com/marketing/7-effective-lead-nurturing-tactics. Accessed April 2021.

One of the common threads that runs through this book is that when you partner your marketing and sales teams, not only will your messaging become more effective, but your marketing team can assist the sales team by capturing and nurturing leads before the leads are passed over to your sales team for closing. Doing so digitally is basically the same as casting a wider net, and it frees up the valuable time of your salespeople to focus on those leads that are ready to be closed.

In this chapter, you will get deeper into the nuts and bolts of the different ways leads are captured, nurtured, and scored (qualified) before being passed along to your sales team for converting.

Why Digital Lead Capture is Important to Distributors

Under typical circumstances, lead capturing and nurturing would be your salesperson's responsibility. But as you know, it's not nearly as easy for a salesperson to interact with prospects as it was a year or two ago. The good news is that your company can leverage marketing automation to support the sales team and actually *capture* and *nurture* that 90% who have been leaving your website without purchasing.

By applying the knowledge you've gained from the first four chapters of this book, you will put your company in a position to successfully focus your sales, marketing, and communications efforts on listening to and understanding your prospects' and customers' needs. From there, you can provide your customers and prospects with the information and answers they are looking for, building their trust, getting them to know, like, and trust you, and drawing them further into your sales funnel.

As you read through Chapter Five, I hope the difference between your simply sharing information versus actual lead capturing and nurturing will become clearer. Lead nurturing requires a certain amount of effort, patience, and a penchant for analytics. We rarely see lead nurturing strategies being used in the distribution industry, and that needs to change. We know from other industries that a well-planned lead nurturing campaign can be both advantageous *and* profitable when correctly executed. Those distributors who put a digital lead capturing and nurturing strategy in place will have a tremendous advantage over those who do not.

In many situations, a lead nurturing strategy will have more success in keeping prospects engaged than the average salesperson would. As your sales funnels lengthen, buyers become more independent, and attention spans shrink. Today's self-directed buyers will navigate through your website like a pinball bouncing from page to page. Unlike the straight-to-the-sale path along which a salesperson would take them, buyers will choose from among several paths leading to the sale.

Because buyers will bounce all over the internet, on and off your website, the chance of your holding their attention from the moment buyers enter your sales cycle to the actual point in which they make a purchase is minimal. It is vital, therefore, to keep visitors engaged 24/7. Even if a sales rep *can* get in front of prospects and customers, he can't babysit them around the clock and so cannot control what they find as they conduct their research.

However, when your website provides your prospects with helpful information, like the information we've already discussed that educates them or that they consider valuable in some other way, you *will* guide them closer to a purchase. Certainly, you would be on the right track, and when you use marketing automation to capture visitors' movements on your site, you will have a much better idea of where your prospects are in your sales funnel, what they're interested in learning more about, and how close they are to a sale.

The goal of lead nurturing is to educate your prospects, build their awareness of your organization and your products and, most importantly, to build their trust in your brand. It is to your advantage to have your prospects and customers know, like, and trust your organization so that they will continue to do business with you.

First Things First: Let's Capture Some Leads!

Before leads can be nurtured, they have got to be captured. So, to get started, let's talk more about some of the more common and successful ways a distributor can begin capturing leads right away.

Capturing Leads Using Content

As discussed in Chapter Three, content that is high quality, valuable, and consistent will generate leads. When you publish blogs, videos, webinars, podcasts, or any other media you create, do your best to publish regularly. It could be once a week, once a month, or any period in between. It just must be consistent.

In most industries, it has become a common practice for B2B companies to capture leads on their websites. A website may offer a free giveaway, such as an eBook, a report, or a newsletter, so that visitors enter their names and email addresses to receive the free giveaway.

We have all seen websites that coax visitors with messages like "Instant Access! Just fill in your name and email address, and we'll send it to you right away!" When crafted well, messages will infer that the visitor will receive something incredibly valuable, and for his convenience, it will be sent directly to their mailbox.

This "free download" method of lead capture was once quite effective, but it has become almost too common in many industries, and today, most people are wise to the tactic. They know that sharing their contact information can possibly result in bothersome spam, so if you're using the "free download" tactic, make it your goal to offer something so attractive and valuable that the reader would be insane to pass it up.

Some less common ways we see companies collecting leads online is by engaging them with interaction. A favorite lead capture tactic of mine is to offer a quiz or an assessment, and today they are easier than ever to create. Prospects seem to enjoy the interactivity of these kinds of tools more than a free download.

Most effective are quizzes and assessments that promise feedback about the reader (people love to learn about themselves) or something that ranks the reader against his peers or competition. Competitive people have a hard time resisting an opportunity to measure themselves against others.

Think back to Joe, the plumber who needed VMI services in Chapter Three. Remember that he had first gone to his plumbing supplier's website and read an article entitled *"Time is Money: Six Tips to Creating a More Efficient Plumbing Business."* When Joe read that article, the plumbing supplier had no idea that Joe had been to their website or that he was looking for a money-saving solution.

Imagine the impact to Joe's buyer's journey if the distributor added a quiz to the end of the article, perhaps something entitled *"Is Your Plumbing Business Leaking Profits? Take This Quiz to Find Out!"* The quiz would have asked two or three questions, and based on Joe's answers, the supplier would know much sooner in the process that Joe needed a solution. They may even have recognized some significant symptoms of his problem and recommended content about VMI programs. Either way, the plumbing supplies distributor would have learned more about Joe's situation much sooner.

Capturing Leads from Social Media

Social media has certainly evolved over the few years it has been around. Capturing leads from social media sites was very easy and basically free at first, and then doing so became difficult and costly. Today it is easy again, but it can be costly.

When social media began to take off around 2009-2010, businesses could set up their presence on their favorite social media sites and run all sorts of contests and giveaways. Back then, businesses enjoyed tremendous exposure.

When a company with a thousand followers posted on their Facebook page, the post would show up in the feed of just about every follower. This phenomenon worked exceptionally well for B2C businesses; and as I'm sure you are aware, it wasn't until several years later that B2B companies jumped into the mix.

Unfortunately, by the time B2Bs began using social media, it was too late for them to capture leads without investing a significant amount of money. Social media companies became publicly traded profit centers, and they quickly put an end to free or low-cost exposure.

Today, a business may have a thousand followers on a social media platform, but only a small handful will see what the business is posting. This is because social media sites use algorithms that make it necessary for companies to pay for exposure or promote their content.

Is it worth it? That's hard to say, but it is certainly worth a try. What's advantageous about promoting your content on social media platforms is that these sites collect massive demographic and firmographic data on their users, giving businesses the ability to laser-target their messaging to a very specific audience.

Capturing Leads Through Referrals

Another way to capture leads is through referrals. Referrals are valuable because they come with a recommendation from a trusted source.

I have a client who is a leadership consultant, and every other Tuesday we publish an article on his behalf and then send an email to his list promoting it. At the bottom of each of these emails we write the following:

PS—If you find this information beneficial, feel free to share. It'll just take a second to forward it to your team or a colleague, and it could improve someone's work habits for a long time to come.

It's a subtle, humble message, and it encourages people to share his content, which results in more eyes looking at his website and eventually signing up to receive more content. It's a very effective tactic and it's an easy way to ask for a referral without putting someone on the spot.

Reviving Old Leads Through Re-Engagement

If you have people on your mailing list who have stopped opening your email, it's possible your mail service will stop delivering to them altogether. Many email programs today recognize an unengaged recipient. Because the reputation of mailing platforms can be negatively impacted by sending to too many unengaged accounts, the platform will take it upon themselves to simply stop delivering to certain accounts.

An easy and effective way to avoid your recipients from becoming unengaged is to run a re-engagement campaign every so often. A re-engagement campaign can be triggered automatically when engagement is very low. It is usually an email with a catchy subject line informing the recipient that he will be removed from your mailing list unless he takes a particular action (such as clicking a link in an email). Sometimes coupons are included in re-engagement campaigns belonging to companies with an eCommerce presence.

Capturing Leads at Live Events

With the advent of COVID-19, many live events were transformed. At first, they came to a screeching halt, and soon after they started occurring through Zoom or other virtual conference or tradeshow software. Virtual or not, events are an excellent way to put yourself in front of a larger audience quickly. They are also among the most effective ways to capture leads.

A live event could be a webinar or an on-line presentation in front of your ideal customer base. It could be a podcast on which you are a guest. It could be a tradeshow where you are operating a breakout room (if virtual) or a booth. It could even be a tradeshow where you are visiting other companies' breakout rooms or booths and interacting with people.

Live events allow you to relate in person, be yourself, demonstrate your knowledge and likeability, learn more about your prospects firsthand, and ask and answer questions directly. Whenever you take part in a live event, be sure to interact with your audience so that they get a stronger sense of who you are and what you represent.

To capture leads at a live event, whether from the stage, in person at a booth, or in a virtual setting, capture the contact information of everyone with whom you engage. A simple sentence like "May I keep in touch with you?" usually does the trick, and their *yes* gives you their permission to add them to your database as a lead and communicate with them digitally (generally via email).

It is worth mentioning that sweepstakes-style contests, such as raffles, are terrific for getting contact information at a live event. People fill out a form that will give you their contact information (usually name, title, company name, email address). Be aware, however, that there are rules in place that require permission to contact entrants after the event. If you'd like to email them, add a small disclaimer to the entry form stating that by entering the drawing they are granting you their permission to contact them.

When you are a paying vendor at a trade show or a speaker at a live event, you contribute value to the organizer. Tap into the law of reciprocity to leverage your contribution by asking the organizer for a list of attendees. Some organizers will share the registration list, but others will not, depending on their policies for sharing contact information and their perception of the value you have contributed.

An even more exciting way to engage with people at a live or virtual event is to ask the organizer for a list of participants *in advance.* Then, a week or so before the event, send the registrants an invitation to connect with you either by visiting your breakout room or booth or introducing themselves following your presentation. Reaching out in advance of an event is an effective first step toward engaging new prospects. It is also an ideal way to distinguish yourself from your competition.

A Few Words About Follow-up

One of the biggest downfalls in the sales arena is our ability to consistently follow-up. Sometimes it seems like there are not enough hours in the day to follow-up the way we'd like to. Time constraint is probably the number one reason companies put automation in place, and follow-up is no different, which is why most companies today will automate their follow-up using marketing automation.

Having said that, though, be aware that people like and expect personalization when they do hear from you, so you *shouldn't* automate a follow-up email for people you've met in person. Rather, you would automate a notification to the sales rep, and the notification can provide him with examples of pre-written messages that he can then personalize and send directly to the recipient himself.

There are instances where automated follow-up is necessary, however. Live events almost always result in a large number of leads to be sorted through, and not every lead can be personalized beyond using someone's first name in the greeting. In a case like this, sort leads by levels of interest, amount of engagement, and whether permission was given to contact them, and then create a strategy for following-up with each segment. In other words, if you met with an individual, whether virtually or in person, you would have a very different follow-up strategy than how you'd follow up with someone who was just another name on a list of attendees you were given.

Best practice dictates that you follow up right away with the people you connect with directly. These are your hot leads. Pick up the phone and call them while you are still top of mind. Then, once you have gone through the list of people you have personally interacted with, follow up with everyone else.

It is important to be mindful about how you follow up with people who did not directly give their permission to contact them. Reaching out en masse via email to a general list can get you into trouble and even get your mail server blackballed, preventing you from sending out group email in the future. If you do want to reach out to a general list via email, your initial communication should begin by asking permission to stay in touch. You do not, however, have to ask permission to contact someone via direct mail or phone call.

Regardless of whether you met a prospect at a live event or you have captured their information in some other way, how do you handle the prospects who are not yet ready to make a purchase? How do you nurture them?

It is helpful to have a plan in place around how often and for how long your salespeople should follow up with their leads. Hopefully, your salespeople have the time and wherewithal to follow your plan, staying in frequent contact with prospects.

Ideally, your salesperson would regularly have a conversation with each prospect to determine their interest. But what if the salesperson drops the ball? Or, what if they cannot get the prospect on the phone or they lose track of the prospect's level of interest? Automated lead nurturing campaigns can help.

Personalization and Lead Nurturing

Personalization and tailored messaging should play a big part in your lead nurturing and follow-up efforts. Remember, your goal is to move prospects closer to a sale, and this is where you have an opportunity to reveal to prospects information about your organization so that they start to know, like, and trust you.

As a reminder, your lead nurturing campaigns are not for telling prospects how great your company is. Instead, use your nurturing sequences to demonstrate how well your company knows your customers and can serve them by touching on their wants, struggles, goals, and pain points. Doing so effectively cannot be accomplished without personalization, by the way.

Once a contact enters your database, your email program and website should have the ability to address them by name. In fact, mailings should always begin with addressing the recipient by their first name. You may have even received mail yourself with your first name in the subject line. It's an effective tactic to get someone's attention.

Have you ever visited a website that greeted you by your first name? Normally, a website knows who you are because you've just logged into it. However, technology has advanced to the point where a website can recognize visitors and call them by name *without* their having to log in. Today, websites will recognize an IP address and cross-reference the IP address to a database. Not only will that allow the website to refer to visitors by name, but it could also display text and images that are relevant to each, giving them a uniquely personalized experience on the site.

Tailored visitor experiences can be industry-specific or dependent on someone's lead score or where the lead is in the sales funnel. The visitor experience can rely on any attribute used to segment an audience.

A cleaning supplies distributor recently found their business growing beyond expectations. Their website was extremely customer-centric, and to their delight, customers quickly became familiar with ordering from their eCommerce site. Over time, the distributor built a section of their website to devote to services and solutions. This area on their website was also getting some traffic.

With all the growth they'd experienced, the distributor wanted to ramp up their recruiting efforts. They had a "Now Hiring" button in the upper right corner of their home page, but the CEO wanted to see messaging that was more conspicuous to better attract quality candidates for their open jobs.

At first, the marketing team built a new home page devoted to their recruiting efforts and quickly started seeing a fair amount of fresh, qualified talent. But they noticed that customer traffic and eCommerce sales were dropping off. They needed a new plan, and so they re-built their home page a second time, giving it the ability to recognize which visitors were customers or prospects and which were job candidates. The update even allowed the distributor's website to identify which industry their customers were visiting from.

As a result of this new change, the distributor's website greeted the recognized institutional customers with images of hospitals, universities, and other facilities similar to those their institutional customers either worked in or served. Its residential contractor customers were greeted with pictures of housing developments and large homes, and similarly their commercial contractor customers were greeted by images of commercial construction. The wording on the page matched the images, and navigation was enhanced to ensure a seamless shopping experience.

When an unrecognized visitor arrived at the site, the visitor was presented with two paths—a path for would-be customers and a path for recruits. If a recruit had already filled out an application and then later returned to the website, the site addressed them by name. The site recognized which pages the candidate had already visited, and it would more heavily promote pages the company wanted the candidate to be sure to see. These changes resulted in a positive outcome for both the company's recruiting efforts and online sales.

Nurturing Leads Using Educational Content

While it is important to share information relevant to the recipient, be careful not to overthink the content creation process. Using information from your *Buyer Persona Worksheets*, begin by creating a series of blog posts that will educate your readers about topics they are interested in. Once you have published the blog posts, you may be able to combine them, along with some images, to create an eBook. When doing so, remember that people are busy, so it is best to keep your messaging succinct and to the point. Use short, simple sentences to hold the reader's attention.

If you confront the reader with lengthy paragraphs, most will skim the text and they may miss important points, so keep paragraphs short. Two programs that are helpful with content creation are Hemingway and Grammarly.

Hemingway will help you better construct your sentences. Hemingway will also give you feedback about the education level at which your content speaks. When it comes to creating blog posts, the rule of thumb is to create content that speaks at the high school level. Regardless of the reader's actual education level, writing at the high school level keeps content easier to read and process quickly, and it will help ensure everyone will benefit from your post.

Grammarly will help with sentence construction and grammar. It is pre-programmable to help you create content that is more business-like, formal, informal, neutral, or conforming to other attributes as well. Grammarly will help you create white papers, eBooks, articles, blog posts and the like. It's available as a free version and a more robust, 'smarter,' paid version. I highly recommend the paid version.

Your readers' perception of your content's value will likely correlate with their perception of your company as a thought leader, so be mindful of production quality. We have all seen white papers and eBooks that looked terrible in terms of their layout, grammar, and typographical errors. Sloppy work is often an indication that the producer doesn't pay attention to detail, which reflects poorly on a business that is trying to gain new customers. Take all steps necessary to ensure your content has a polished, professional look and feel.

Look at the analytics for each piece of content you publish. Notice who is reading your material and who is not. Do some social listening (described below) and research to be sure the content is focusing on relevant subject matter. Look at what people are clicking on or reading or liking on social media.

Nurturing Leads Through Content Mapping

When your sales funnel is built out with valuable content, it will nurture your leads toward a sale. The purpose of content mapping is to increase the velocity of a lead's journey through that funnel. It's essential to keep a close eye on your leads, adjusting your funnel to accommodate the unexpected, and being mindful that your leads aren't going off track or stalling. The reporting functions in your marketing automation system will help to monitor your funnels.

Here is an example of a simple sales funnel with content mapping. Note how prospects are moved from the top of the funnel to the bottom of the funnel using content and calls to action (CTA).

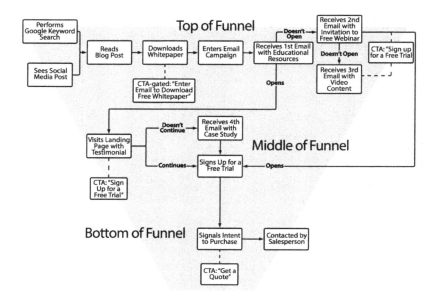

In Chapter Three with Joe the plumber, we used content mapping to move Joe from his original thought about needing a time-management program to realizing he needed a better way to manage his inventory.

Lead Monitoring Using Social Media

Monitoring social media, also known as social listening, is another way to keep tabs on and nurture your leads. Social listening is the process of setting up alerts on your social media channel for mentions of your brand, your competition, your products, your solutions, and more. When someone mentions a word or phrase you're monitoring for, you can easily join the conversation and lead them towards your company, one of your salespeople, and possibly a purchase.

Through social listening your sales and marketing teams can track, analyze, and even respond to conversations on social media. It is a crucial component of audience research and lead nurturing because it puts you directly in touch with what your customers and prospects are looking for.

Most off-the-shelf social media programs provide the tools necessary to succeed in social listening. It is as easy as adding keywords to your platform, and then every time someone mentions that keyword, you are alerted as to who made the mention and the context in which it was shared. In fact, some social listening programs offer the ability to track leads in real-time as they interact across social media channels.

If Joe the plumber posted on Twitter or Facebook asking colleagues for ideas about inventory management, and the plumbing distributor was monitoring for the keyword phrase 'inventory management', the distributor would have spotted Joe's inquiry right away and given him a call.

Lead Scoring: Your Secret Weapon to an Increase in Sales

To understand the process of nurturing a lead and taking it from an MQL (marketing-qualified lead) to an SQL (sales-qualified lead), it is helpful to have a clear plan for and understanding of your lead-scoring process. Lead scoring is the practice of ranking the value of captured leads. It is essential in determining a lead's sales-readiness. Lead scoring is not a replacement for account engagement, however. It is simply a method to help the sales team rank and prioritize leads.

Simply put, lead scoring measures two main components of your buyers:

- How each buyer fits into your ideal customer profile
- A buyer's behaviors that indicate interest in a product or service

The best lead scoring systems capture demographic and firmographic attributes, including company size, job title, location, revenue, as well as number of clicks, pages visited, media downloaded, time spent on web pages, keywords searched on, and so much more.

Lead scoring relies upon the ability to track a prospect's actions, which could include clicking through an email, interacting with your content, spending time on your website, liking or commenting on your social media posts, and much more. It then assigns point values based on those behaviors as well as a lead's decision-making authority, title, company location, revenue, and any other attributes that would help determine their candidacy as a customer.

When it comes to lead scoring, the sales department ultimately decides a lead's value, but the marketing team must fully understand that value so they can chart the path a lead will take to get the lead sales-ready. Together the two teams will measure and assign scores to behaviors displayed and actions taken that stem from the sales and marketing collateral contained within your sales funnels until those numbers hit a high enough score to be passed over to sales.

Let's say you are an HVAC distributor, and a prospect visits your website and signs up for your newsletter. That action is assigned a value of 5, meaning 5 points get added to their lead score. Soon after, that prospect visits three different product pages featuring low-cost items. If each low-cost item's page visit is given a value of 5 as well, the prospect's score goes up to 20. If you were to ask the sales team whether they would like to work this lead, their answer would hopefully be "not yet."

A few days later, the same prospect returns to your website, and this time the prospect is looking at a page in the Solutions area that promotes a service that is very profitable for your business. An initial visit to that page may be assigned a value of 25, thus bumping their score up to 45. Would it be time for a salesperson to reach out to them? Perhaps not just yet. But, let's assume that on that same page is a 3-question quiz related to that solution. Let's also assume the prospect takes the quiz, entering their name and email address. Now comes the fun part.

For starting the quiz, you might assign a value of 20 and then add a value of 20 for each answer the prospect selects that would indicate their suitability as a candidate for this service. The first question might ask about the size of their organization. The second question might ask about their HVAC area of expertise (e.g., small residential vs. large commercial). The third might ask about their location. At this point, by giving all the "right" answers on the quiz, the prospect's lead score might bump up to over 100. If, at this point, you ask the sales team whether they want this lead, their answer is sure to be a resounding, "Yes!"

Timing is also a factor when setting up your lead scoring. A salesperson may request a lead be passed on to him after the lead downloads and opens four pieces of content. That sounds reasonable, but if the prospect opened and downloaded those four items over the past three years, is he really a valuable prospect? Possibly not. Your lead-scoring formula should contain an aging process to accommodate such situations. Over time a score will go down, indicating waning interest. Likewise, as new actions take place, a score will go up.

Lead scoring is an ongoing process that the sales and marketing teams should review regularly. When your salespeople share information about the sales cycle with the marketing team, the marketing team can then create and map your content inside your sales funnel to meet the parameters of your lead scoring process.

To put a lead scoring program in place, it will be necessary for your organization to have a marketing automation system with tracking capability as well as lead scoring capability. Using your system, your sales and marketing teams would decide on and preload all the criteria and attributions you would like to measure and have contribute to a prospect's lead score. The marketing automation system will calculate the scores for you and, based on a prospect hitting certain scores, would trigger different events.

In the example above, when a prospect hits the score of 100, your marketing automation system would trigger a notification to a salesperson to take control of the lead. The marketing automation system might also change the prospect's status from a Contact to a Lead or a Lead to an Opportunity.

Now it's your turn. In your supplemental materials you will find an *Attributes Checklist* and a *Lead Scoring Worksheet*. Check off the attributes that your salespeople (with the help of the marketing team) would like to score their leads based on. Once you have all agreed on that list of attributes, add each attribute to the *Lead Scoring Worksheet* and rank them from Critical, Important, Influential, and Negative. You will find directions for completing both forms on the forms themselves.

Visit MDM.com/TDDBook to download the Worksheets, Checklists, Agendas, Guidebooks, etc. referred to in this book.

CHAPTER 6

What to Measure, How to Succeed

"Leading organizations are moving toward "full-funnel" marketing, an approach that combines the power of both brand building and performance marketing through linked teams, measurement systems, and key performance indicators (KPIs). By adopting full-funnel marketing, companies can become more relevant to their customers, develop a fuller and more accurate picture of marketing's overall effectiveness, and generate more value without having to spend additional marketing dollars. This approach isn't just about doing more across each stage of the funnel. It's about understanding how each of the stages impacts the others for a complete customer experience—how media spend on addressable TV, for example, can boost the impact of personalized emails, or how social-media ad campaigns can drive online and in-store visits.

In our experience, a thoughtful and data-driven full-funnel marketing strategy can drive significant value. By shifting greater media allocation to areas with higher returns and employing test-and-learn optimization for demand-generation campaigns, marketers can achieve a 15 to 20 percent lift in marketing ROI."[11]

It used to be that digital marketing was measured by what has been coined 'soft metrics,' such as brand awareness, impressions, open rates, click-through rates, new vs. repeat traffic, search rankings and the like. While soft metrics are important, what really matters at the end of the day is the impact to your bottom line.

Soft metrics will provide you with insight into whether your digital efforts are working. For example, if the click-through rate on an email you send is very low, you may not see any impact to your business's bottom line; but knowing that the click-through rate is low is helpful in that you could tie that metric back to an email that simply does not resonate. The same can be said for other soft metrics such as the ones mentioned in the paragraph above. Measuring soft metrics as you begin this part of your digital sales transformation journey is helpful because it will allow you to tweak the effectiveness of every step in your sales funnels and content marketing efforts.

As you measure the activity inside your funnels, you will be able to measure each element of the buyer's journey, identify the activities that generate the best results, and eliminate or modify the ineffective parts of your campaigns. Marketing automation tools with robust reporting capabilities will allow your teams to confidently analyze their findings and adjust where necessary.

From there, you will continue to measure based on a decided timeframe and determine whether there is measurable growth, and

---

11 Ader, Jacob, Boudet, Julien, Brodherson, Marc, and Robinson, Kelsey. "Why Every Business Needs a Full-Funnel Marketing Strategy." *McKinsey & Company.* February 12, 2021. https://www.mckinsey.com/business-functions/marketing-and-sales/our-insights/why-every-business-needs-a-full-funnel-marketing-strategy. Accessed April 2021.

if that growth is consistent. If so, stick with what you are doing. If not, see what could have been done differently, and focus on the improvements that deliver the best long-term results.

Taking Steps for Improvement

There are several areas to review when you are not seeing the results you desire or expect with your soft metrics. Poor results could be due to any of the following issues, or a combination of two or more. Adjust each issue and test the results to isolate the problem to the best of your ability.

- **Keywords:** Try new keywords or variations of keywords to see if they help your content get found more often. Since each page on your company's website can incorporate different keywords, keyword testing is not difficult to do.

- **Search Engine Optimization (SEO):** See if changing a simple on-page SEO factor can help boost visits. Examples of on-page factors are page title, meta description, and headings. As a simple test, try changing the page title of one of your key web pages to see if more traffic is generated.

- **Conversion Tactics:** Try new design ideas with your lead capture forms or landing pages. Make a change to the layout of a page by moving the form's placement, or use an image that is completely different from what is there currently. Try different colors and different fonts, different images, and different calls-to-action. You'll find that sometimes even the slightest changes will boost conversion results.

- **Content:** Determine which content is bringing your website the most traffic and leads. Focus on generating more on that kind of content or refine your promotion of other content pieces or modes to match what is working well.

- **Social Media:** Evaluate which social media channels are generating the most website visitors and leads. Again, either focus on your successful social media platforms, or try improving your performance in your less successful channels.

- **Lead Nurturing and Email Marketing:** Maybe your marketing team is mailing too frequently or not frequently enough. Maybe the calls-to-action your company is using are not attractive to your audience. Keep experimenting and testing.

The Impact to Your Bottom Line

> *"Revenue attribution is a tough issue to scope out. But it's well worth the effort. Forrester research analyst Tina Moffett states, "B2B companies are seeing an average of 15 to 18 percent lift in revenue as a result of implementing a closed-loop attribution system and then optimizing marketing programs based on the more sophisticated analysis. The size of the prize, a 15 to 18 percent lift, makes revenue attribution worth pursuing. That's a game changer."[12]*

Your digital strategy can and should be measured by its ability to contribute to the growth of your sales pipeline, helping to drive revenue and profit. With a strong digital sales and marketing strategy that delivers trackable data, in many cases you will be able to confidently tie your digital efforts directly to an increase in your company's growth.

Once you are comfortable with your soft metrics, and everything is in place and working well, take steps to gather a more-informed view of how your digital sales and marketing efforts are performing. You'll find you will begin to develop a stronger ability to forecast what to expect in future quarters and years.

---

12 "How Top CMOs Quantify Marketing Investment with Revenue Attribution." *Sales Benchmark Index (SBI)*, September 6, 2017. https://salesbenchmarkindex.com/insights/piloting-revenue-attribution-how-top-cmos-quantify-marketing-impact/ Accessed April 2021.

By taking a revenue-focused approach to what we have discussed and put in place thus far, you will be able to justify your investment and see how your marketing efforts have contributed and will continue to contribute to your company's revenue.

The following metrics are the ones to focus on when measuring the outcome of each campaign and analyzing ROI.

- **Number of New Leads / Cost Per Lead:** Simply put, new leads are the prospects brought in by a digital campaign, but it is important to note that not all leads are valuable. Your goal for new leads is to nurture them into MQLs and SQLs.

- **Number of Marketing Qualified Leads (MQLs):** MQLs are leads who have completed a relevant action (such as clicked through an email) and who meet a certain lead score threshold. They may or may not be warm just yet, so MQLs are not ready to be passed on to sales. Instead, MQLs should reside in a nurturing cycle until their score hits the SQL level.

- **Number of Sales Qualified Leads (SQLs):** SQLs are leads who hit the next lead score threshold beyond MQL and are confirmed to be warm or hot, and they should be passed on to the sales team for handling.

- **Number of New Opportunities / Cost Per Opportunity:** Opportunities are the leads who show a possible intent to buy. If someone qualifies as an opportunity, it means a sales account executive thinks the lead might become a closed-won deal with an associated dollar amount.

- **Effectiveness by Channel:** Has interaction increased on social media channels? Through webinars or other events? Through referrals or loyalty programs? What is working more effectively? What promotion channels or referring sources are sending the best traffic? Focus on long-term, consistent results here, not short-term traffic spurts.

- **Customer Acquisition Cost:** A little tougher to measure, but if you are spending money on advertising, trade shows, and direct mail, put indicators in place that will track how customers found you and the path they took to become a customer. Keep track of how much you are investing to draw in each new customer. If you rely primarily on outbound marketing methods, your cost per customer acquisition is probably higher than it could or should be.

Once you have a handle on the more significant, 'hard' metrics above, you can tie them directly to how each have affected your bottom line by their impact on the following metrics:

- **Sales Lift / Sales Conversion** – How many of the leads acquired through your digital efforts became customers?

- **Average Order Value** – Of the new leads acquired, what was their average order value? Of your existing customers, has any of their behavior or activity on your website led to new sales?

- **Revenue Growth** – How much of your revenue growth can be tied back to customers acquired via your digital efforts?

- **Customer Lifetime Value** – Have you extended your customers' lifetime value through stronger retention programs during the loyalty stage of the buyer's journey? How does this translate into dollars and cents?

In your supplemental materials you will find a *KPI Tracking Worksheet*. Use this worksheet to track the progress of your KPIs, both good and bad. This will help you isolate anomalies and get a better understanding of what your audience responds to.

Visit MDM.com/TDDBook to download the Worksheets, Checklists, Agendas, Guidebooks, etc. referred to in this book.

Drivers of a Successful Digital Transformation

Only about 30% of companies navigate a digital transformation successfully. And navigating it in the midst of uncertainty—the new reality—is especially difficult because new behaviors and expectations take shape and evolve at warp speed.

It doesn't happen in one fell swoop. Transformations succeed when they are incremental, cost-effective, and sustainable. That means focusing on outcomes: new products, improved processes, and other use cases that, one by one, let you build capabilities, business value, and buy-in for the transformation.[13]

Depending on where you conduct your research, you'll find information from dozens of leading consultants who tell us there are anywhere from two to twenty-one critical factors to a successful digital transformation.

---

13 Boston Consulting Group on Digital Transformation https://www.bcg.com/capabilities/digital-technology-data/digital-transformation/ Accessed September 2021.

Despite the widely varying number of critical factors mentioned in the research I've come across, the six below from Boston Consulting Group collectively sum things up quite nicely. They are:

1. Craft an integrated strategy with clear goals and a definition of success.
2. Have one-hundred percent commitment from leadership from the very top (C-Suite) through middle management.
3. Put the best employees in the right positions, ensuring a good mix of digital expertise and organizational experience.
4. Adopt an agile governance mindset and culture throughout the organization.
5. Aim for interoperable, business-driven, modular, and flexible technology.
6. Monitor and measure your progress against the goals set in number one above.

BCG's material rightly states that companies who follow the six keys above will more than triple their likelihood of success.

This is a lot for an organization to undertake, but the good news is that you only must go through the really difficult parts one time if you do a thorough job of it. With that in mind, here are some parting words of wisdom that I've picked up along the way during my years of working with distributors.

Don't Lose Sight of Your Customers

It's easy to lose sight of your customers when going through any transformation, let alone one of such great magnitude. But, unfortunately, what's even more likely to happen when caught up in such distracting activities is that your customers may lose sight of *you*. You cannot let that happen.

Taking quick action on what we've shared throughout the pages of this book will help ensure the focus of your customers and prospects is on you. Follow the steps we've laid out for you, and you'll meet your customers where they're at and on their terms. You'll stay in front of them, remain top of mind, and have a much greater chance at showing customers and prospects that your distributorship is in the 'helping' business.

Keep in mind that buyers everywhere have come to expect a certain level of targeted, personalized communication from their vendors, including you. Personalized communication reinforces a customer's belief that you know them, understand them, and have their best interests at heart. Personalization also means NOT sending information to customers that doesn't pertain to them. By segmenting your audience, one of the first steps we've covered, you can make it clear that your company understands its customers, would make an excellent partner, and therefore should be each individual segment's supplier of choice.

Similarly, segments of your buyers are scattered throughout your sales cycle, each navigating their way through their buyer's journey toward a purchase with your company. Buyers today are self-directed, no longer following a predictable or linear path. Knowing *where* your buyers are in their journey, *who* they are, and *what* they're looking for will give you a more holistic view of them (remember Adobe and Salesforce's goal of giving you a 360-degree view of your customers). You'll have a better ability to meet your customers and prospects wherever they are in your digital sales cycle.

Think Like Your Customers Think

When a customer engages with a sales rep, the sales rep listens to the customer, then says what he must to move the customer closer to a purchase. In many situations, your digital content can do the same.

People who turn to the internet for answers are interested in finding solutions to specific problems. To ensure your prospects and customers discover *your* solutions, describe your solutions in ways that include specific references to the issues your buyers are searching on. Buyers will click on and read information that sounds as though it is about themselves or a company like them, especially a company that has suffered from and found a resolution to a problem like their own.

But buyers cannot search for a solution they're unaware of, and they won't recognize a solution as being for them if it doesn't speak directly to their problem. Today's buyers are self-directed, and they'll direct themselves to digital collateral that speaks about the issues they care about, i.e., the information they're searching for. They're not interested in information about how great your company is, so if you'd like to lead your buyers toward your solutions and closer to a sale, publish the same information your salespeople would share when they're face-to-face with a customer – information that is tailored to the customers' needs and wants.

You want to generate new leads — doing so is vital to growing your business. To do so in a way where you can turn those leads into buyers, consider how people shop. When a buyer walks into a store, he'll often do all he can to avoid a salesperson until he has gathered enough information on his own. When a salesperson approaches too soon, you'll hear the familiar *"Can I help you?"* followed by *"No thanks. I'm just looking."*

A seasoned salesperson will likely hang back and wait and watch. If the customer spends a lot of time near the trousers, that's a hint to the salesperson that he may be interested in purchasing some trousers. If the customer takes some trousers into a dressing room, the salesperson learns even more about what he'd like to purchase. Then, when the customer asks whether the trousers come in blue — bingo! The game is afoot, and the salesperson's job begins.

Today, people conduct their B2B shopping much the same as how they shop as a consumer. Using marketing automation and your CRM, your salespeople can do with your leads what the salesperson above did with his customer. Your salespeople can 'hang back and watch' where customers and prospects spend their time online. They can observe and keep track of the products and services each buyer interacts with most. They can also monitor behavior and receive activity notifications that indicate the buyer is close to a purchase.

You can never take for granted that your customers know everything you do or every way you can serve them. The example above suggests that customers aren't interested in your help until they realize they need it. So, you must let it be known how you can solve their problems by sharing content about all the issues your solutions can solve. You also must share your digital collateral as widely and as often as possible in multiple ways using various media formats. By doing so, you can reach bigger audiences and develop more effective ways to speak directly to each segment at each stage in the buyer's journey.

Build it, Measure it, Rinse, and Repeat

One of the most significant benefits of a digital transformation is that anything and everything is measurable, flexible, and can be improved upon. So, think of every step you take in your digital transformation as another step in your new sales flywheel where you can gauge what works and what doesn't. Along the way, there may be a new strategy or tactic to consider, and whether it is better or more effective will only be known by monitoring and measuring your increased or decreased success.

When you see a strategy that works well, you can do more of the winning strategy and apply the strategy to future sales and marketing activities. If a strategy or tactic doesn't work, you can zero in on exactly what didn't work and then adjust it to make it better. But you'll never have to start over from scratch. Your 'sales machine' will be built, and it will only get better.

Pay Attention to Your Communication

If or when your products become more widely accessible from other sources, and your customers are presented with new choices, it's crucial that your company maintain the perception that the customer's smartest move is to continue purchasing from you. The better your ability to communicate and demonstrate to your customers how much value they're getting by being your customer, the less likely you'll be pulled into a price war. Your battle for customer wallet share will lessen, too, as you improve your ability to succinctly communicate that you understand and can fulfill your customers' needs.

And communicate you must. Today's buyers will dig deep into your internet presence to learn everything they possibly can about your organization. Always clarify the value your company offers by highlighting the benefits to the customer in everything you publish. Surely your customers gain certain advantages from partnering with you.

Advantages might include access to more advanced technology and buying history, more straightforward ordering procedures, or quicker and more frequent deliveries. Highlight those advantages in such a way that customers and prospects will recognize your business as well-equipped and the obvious choice to deliver the value they need and want.

Create a Winning Team with an Eye Toward the Future

The steps in this book are only possible when your marketing and sales functions are aligned. Your marketing team should have the know-how and digital prowess to put the necessary activities in motion, but they will need full cooperation and guidance from the sales team to get the messaging right. In addition, the sales team will only benefit from sharing their insights about your customer segments, their pain points, what appeals to them, and what each segment truly wants and has come to expect. So, it's in their best interest to be forthcoming with their information and keep patient with the process.

After all, your salespeople have had a front-row seat to your customer base for many years and have been trained to quickly assess a customer's needs, perhaps within a two-to-three-minute conversation. In contrast, your marketing team has six or seven seconds to grab a buyer's attention, let alone move him closer to a sale. The more your marketers learn about your customers and how to appeal to them, the better a chance they will have to capture or advance a lead.

You may find some of the processes we've included to be complex (because some of them really are). The worksheets and other tools provided will help your team move more seamlessly through the steps and keep essential information organized.

Many of the activities will only have to be tackled once. Then as you implement the accompanying strategies the processes lead to, you'll be positioning your company for a smoother and more innovative future.

You will have a much stronger foundation on which to maintain a solid foothold in your industry, and you will remain fully prepared to continuously communicate your value and compete in the digital space. In addition, you will be far better prepared to conquer whatever new and exciting digital advancements or improvements the future brings.